FAILED
TO
RETURN

FAILED TO RETURN

The Yorkshire Memorials to the Bomber Squadrons of No.4 Group RAF and No.6 (RCAF) Group, 1939-1945

Bill Norman

LEO COOPER
LONDON

First published in Great Britain in 1995 by Leo Cooper
190 Shaftesbury Avenue, London WC2H 8JL
an imprint of Pen & Sword Books Limited
47 Church Street, Barnsley, South Yorkshire S70 2AS

*For up-to-date information on other titles produced under
the Leo Cooper imprint, please telephone or write to:*
    Pen & Sword Books Ltd
    FREEPOST
    47 Church Street
    Barnsley
    South Yorkshire S70 2BR
Telephone (24 hours): 01226 734555

ISBN 0 85052 474 1

British Library Cataloguing in Publication Data

Designed and produced by Wharncliffe Publishing Limited (Book Division)

Printed by Redwood Books Ltd
Trowbridge, Wiltshire

The Astronomical Clock Memorial, in the north transept of York Minster, commemorates the airmen of Britain, the Commonwealth and Allied countries who lost their lives during the Second World War while operating from airfields in the northern counties of Yorkshire, Durham and Northumberland.

The Roll of Honour in the glass-topped case below the clock face contains the names of some 18,000 officers and men who served with Bomber, Fighter and Coastal Commands and who failed to return from operations. Thus, the memorial does not commemorate only those crews who flew with No.4 Group and No.6 (RCAF)Group, but the names of men – including 3,537 Canadians – who flew with the Yorkshire bomber squadrons are in the majority in the Book of Remembrance.

The idea for such a memorial was suggested by the Royal British Legion and was supported by the Royal Air Force Association. The cost was met by public subscription, following a joint appeal.

The clock was designed in the early 1950s by Dr R.d'E. Atkinson (of the Royal Greenwich Observatory), while the case and its structure were conceived by Professor Sir Albert Richardson (President of the Royal Academy). The memorial was dedicated in 1955, in the presence of HRH the Duke of Edinburgh.

This book is dedicated to all crews of the Royal Air Force Bomber Command who served during the Second World War, and particularly to those who failed to return.

We will remember them

TO AN ABSENT FRIEND

Take down his coat,
Pack up his things -
The scribbled note,
The tunic with wings;
The books, cricket pads and bat,
And his beloved misshapen hat.

Auction his car,
Attend to his debts,
And then there are
His several pets -
The Tortoise, Collie dog and Bird
Whose cheerful chirp is now unheard.

No more kissing
Or popsies thrilled;
He's reported 'Missing,
Believed killed'.
He had no ribbons, won no fame,
We'll toast his memory just the same.

Squadron Leader Vernon Noble, 4 Group, 1942

CONTENTS

Stonefall RAF cemetery, Harrogate. The Cross of Sacrifice that stands in the background was unveiled by His Excellency the High Commissioner of Canada, Mr L.D. Wilgress, in July 1951. At the time of the unveiling, the plot contained the graves of 994 Service personnel, mostly airmen. These included 23 New Zealanders, 97 Australians, 170 Britons and 665 Canadians. It was because of the preponderance of Canadians in Stonefall that the unveiling was performed by a representative from Canada; it also explains why so many of the trees there are maples.

INTRODUCTION

Although this is a book about the Yorkshire memorials to the Bomber Command squadrons of No.4 Group Royal Air Force and No.6 Group Royal Canadian Air Force, its purpose is not simply to list the many monuments which have been erected throughout the county during the last decade: the text also includes details of the squadrons commemorated and the grievous losses they sustained, both in operations and in training.

My principal intention in compiling this volume is to encourage readers to seek out these memorials, and when they do, to 'look beyond' the stone; to realise the multiplicity of dangers that bomber crews faced and to appreciate the courage they displayed, not especially in conspicuous acts of bravery − though there were many of those − but simply in their efforts to survive a 'tour' of thirty operations, when the statistical chances of their doing so were often less than one in six. To this end, the details of each memorial are accompanied by at least one tale of a 'dicey' trip or a crew lost.

The following pages contain a number of stories relating to aircrew who operated from Yorkshire half a century ago, but the reader will find little mention of the 'famous' men of Bomber Command. However, this is a book about heroes; a book about boys 'whom war made men long before their time', and who took to the skies in the knowledge that Chance was not on their side.

It is worth remembering that all of the men who flew with Bomber Command during the Second World War were volunteers, each aiming to carry out thirty operations to complete a first 'tour of duty' before embarking upon a second tour of twenty trips after a six months' rest . However, the chances favouring completion of even one tour were very slim indeed. In the black days of 1942-43 some squadrons were losing aircraft at the rate of 5 per cent per operation, which meant that all crews would have 'got the chop' before completing even twenty trips, let alone their first thirty; the odds favouring the completion of two tours were even lower.

Bomber crews had to deal with death on a regular basis and the dangers came in many forms: from crashes while attempting to take off, fully laden with bomb load and fuel; from ice, which was capable of forming in such weight and extent that it could immobilize control surfaces and flip an aircraft into a spin from which there would be little chance of escape; from the nightfighter and from flak, each with its threat of withering shrapnel, fiery incandescence or explosive obliteration; from bombs dropped by higher flying 'friendly' aircraft as the bombing force crossed the target area in layers to reduce time in the danger zone − a strategy of congestion which always carried the additional hazard of collision; from having to bale out, often in a concentrated bomber stream and over a blazing target area where the air was filled with the bullets of intercepting nightfighters and the deadly debris of exploding shells; from the need to 'ditch', having survived the maelstrom of the bombing run, and to chance one's luck in the gray waters of the North Sea or the English Channel; from the further risk of collision on return to base as multitudes of aircraft circled in overlapping landing circuits caused by the close proximity of airfields; and from crashing on touch-down, having suffered battle damage and on the homeward trip having successfully met every challenge − except the final one.

Each of those dangers made its separate contribution to the overall losses. During 1939-45 the aircrews of RAF Bomber Command flew a total of 389,809 operational sorties (on the basis of the best estimates available) from which 8,953 aircraft failed to return: a loss rate of 2.3 per cent. A further 1,368 aircraft crashed in this country while setting off on operations or returning from them.

In Yorkshire, No.4 Group lost at least 1,509 aircraft on operations, with an additional (unknown) number lost in crashes ; the total losses for No.6 Group amounted to 1,289 aircraft. What such losses represent in terms of aircrew cannot be given with any degree of precision, although an estimate would suggest some 14,000 casualties.

Of the 125,000 aircrew who served with the squadrons and training units of Bomber Command during 1939-1945, 73,741 (59.1 per cent) became casualties [the highest loss rate sustained by any arm of the British Armed Forces during the Second World War] 55,573 (44.4per cent) of whom were killed[1]. A number of those who died now rest in graveyards throughout the United Kingdom, but most laid down their lives much further afield and lie buried in the war cemeteries of Europe or have no known grave. Those bomber crews classified as 'Missing on operations' are listed among the 20,466 names carved on the Air Forces Memorial at Runnymede. Most of those who died were members of the Royal Air Force, but contingents from the Commonwealth also bore their share of the losses[2].

In the face of such carnage it is hardly surprising that superstition played an important part in maintaining a flyer's morale. Many aircrew carried their mascots and their lucky charms as safeguards against danger, while others had deliberately set patterns in the way they prepared for operations: never changing; always exactly the same; and always rooted in the belief that what had kept them safe in the past would do so in the future − although, sadly, subsequent events were often to prove otherwise.

Bombing up, 1942. (Northern Echo)

Perhaps, even now, the sacrifice made by those thousands of young men has yet to receive the recognition it deserves. For most people of that generation the Second Wold War is a distant memory, but those who were there and who survived relatively unscathed have not forgotten. Since the end of the Second World War many veterans have been drawn to re-visit their old war-time stations and to remember, often with pain, days long gone and friends once known. But such pilgrimages often bring disappointment.

Many of the northern airfields from which bombers were launched to attack targets in Occupied Europe some fifty years ago now lie derelict; gradually succumbing to Nature's inexorable advance. Others have long since been erased as the land on which they once stood has been returned to former uses. With the passing of each year, the abandoned airfields that remain descend deeper into anonymity and show a little less to nudge the memory. Soon nothing will remain to remind even the curious passer-by of the dramas that were enacted there; nothing to tell of the courage and endurance of crews who took to the skies and faced every danger; nothing to prompt an appreciation of the magnitude of their sacrifice.

In 1958, when ex-navigator Don Charlwood (author of the Bomber Command classic, *No Moon Tonight*) revisited the Lincolnshire airfield at Elsham Wolds, from where he flew his tour of operations, he found that:

'..the guardhouse and the sick-quarters were in ruins, overgrown with nettles...Most of the dispersed Nissen huts had gone, but I had the illusion that in the intact buildings ahead there must yet be men, or at least a sign left for me... I went in at the open door..anticipating the smell of beer and bacon and wet greatcoats, the sound of voices. But down the long room (of the Mess) lay ploughs and harrows and bags of superphosphate. The windows were obscured with dust and cobwebs; the cheap lining of the ceiling hung in tatters...

I stood very still. Somewhere hens were clucking and rain gurgled off a roof. There were no other sounds at all. Something in the room eluded me; a deafness shut me from messages on the dusty air. I walked quickly into the rain, groping for understanding of our silenced activity, the purpose of all the courage and devotion I had once seen. I reached the car wet and cold. Rain was falling steadily, but I stood for a long time, casting about again for some signs of all the comradeship and courage that had ennobled this tattered hill. At the gate I felt an urge to write across the decaying columns: 'Here was the home of 103 Squadron, RAF Bomber Command, 1941-45.'

Thirty-six years after Charlwood made his visit, virtually all trace of the airfield at Elsham Wolds has disappeared.

It is this need to seek affirmation of the comradeship, the courage, the devotion to duty, and particularly the losses sustained by bomber crews during the last war that has resulted in the spread of memorials to No.4 Group RAF and No.6 Group RCAF throughout Yorkshire during the last decade.

During that time, twenty-three such monuments have been erected in the county, usually close by the sites of war-time airfields. Generally speaking, the initiative has come from Squadron Associations, but some memorials owe their existence to private individuals who have felt driven to make their own gesture to the memory of men they never knew, but with whom they feel an affinity. The following pages address them all.

In recent years, aspects of the air war against Occupied Europe have been much criticized by people of a later generation far removed from the dangerous days of 1939-45 and well served by the benefits of hindsight. They point to the casualties inflicted by the Allied bombing policy, devised by strategists and sanctioned by politicians, and they level the charge against the crews who implemented it.

In the light of such accusations, it should be remembered that at the time when this island stood alone against an evil régime and was facing catastrophes on every front, when our cities were being subjected to attacks by the *Luftwaffe*, when the Battle of the Atlantic was threatening

RAF Snaith, now an industrial estate, June 1994.

our national survival, and at the time when the Nazis were inflicting suffering on an appalling scale throughout Continental Europe, the bomber offensive was the only means that Britain had to show its defiance and at the same time cause the diversion of at least some of Germany's offensive resources of arms and men to a defensive role (aimed at the protection of its towns and cities).

The men of Bomber Command carried out what they perceived to be their duty with great fortitude − and at a cost which should never be forgotten. Sometimes, no doubt, even those who survived will question the purpose of it all, and the answer will not always come readily. But in the black days of the Second World War, the sight of Bomber Command setting out night after night kept national morale steady and strengthened the will to carry on. As Max Hastings has pointed out[3], 'The enthusiastic publicity accorded to the bomber offensive was to play an important part in keeping hope alive among the British people until at least June, 1944.' If that hope had faded perhaps the history of the western world would be rather different from what it is today.

The men who flew with Bomber Command fifty years ago stoically faced death and destruction at almost every turn and they did what a grateful nation expected of them. It is in the nature of international conflict that nations demand that citizens 'do their duty' in what ever shape or form that may be − but Humanity pays the price. Casualties were inflicted on a catastrophic scale by both sides during the last war, and combatants and civilians alike became the pawns of Time and circumstance, subjected to − and moulded by − the imperatives of the moment. Thus, if men must seek to assign retrospective blame or guilt for acts of war, then let them blame War itself − for it is indeed a brutal and brutalising social activity which allows no victors but which ultimately makes victims of us all.

Notes

1. Fatal casualties: 55,573(44.4%); prisoners of war: 9,838(7.9%); wounded, other than prisoners of war: 8,403(6.8%). Total casualties: 73,741(59.1%)
2. Royal Air Force 38,462(69.2%); Royal Canadian Air Force 9,919(17.2%); Royal Australian Air Force 4,050(7.3%); Royal New Zealand Air Force 1,679(3.0%); other Allied air forces 1,463(2.7%).
3. Max Hastings(1980)

ACKNOWLEDGEMENTS

Particular thanks to Squadron Leader Don Hibbert, DFC DFM RAF (Retd) ex-10/158 Squadrons, for help generously given on a whole range of relevant issues. Special mention must also be given to Martin Middlebrook's and Chris Everitt's *The Bomber Command War Diaries* (1990 ed), which has been the principal source of squadron loss statistics except where otherwise stated.

Charles Adams DFM ex-578 Squadron; Mrs Sheila Barnett; Uwe Benkel, Kaiserslautern, Germany; Mrs D. Booth and No.10 Squadron Association for permission to use Bill Booth's article *Free Fall*; Charlie Brister, ex-77 Squadron, for permission to use his account of his bale-out on the Berlin raid 23 August 1943; Squadron Leader Harry Coates DFC, ex-640 Squadron for the loan of the record of 640 Squadron operations and losses; Lieutenant Colonel R. Brousseau, 433 Squadron RCAF; Group Captain Dudley Burnside, DSO OBE DFC, ex-427 (Lion) Squadron,RCAF; Maurice Burtoft, ex-433 (Porcupine) Squadron,RCAF; Lawrence Caffery; Ron Cassels, ex-428 (Ghost) Squadron, for permission to quote from his memoir *Ghost Squadron*; Commonwealth War Graves Commission; Peter Clowes, for the extract from *The Last Flight of Halifax MZ831Z*; Norman Davidson; Ken Dean DFC ex-51 Squadron; Laurent Dufresne, ex-433 (Porcupine) Squadron,RCAF; Group Captain. Ivor Easton RAF (Ret'd) and Gerald Carver, ex-78 Squadron; Jim Feaver DFC ex-51 Squadron; Jack Fitzsimmons, Canada; Keith Ford, ex-51 Squadron; Dorien Freeman, 158 Squadron Association; George French, 76 Squadron Association H.N. Gill. 51 Squadron Association; Brian Gillard; Chris Goss; Ernie Hardy, for research at the PRO; Stephen Harper; Maurice Hepworth, ex-640 Squadron; Stan Jeffrey, ex-102 Squadron; Len Jewsbury, ex-10 Squadron; Jim Kinder, ex-433 (Porcupine) Squadron,RCAF, for details of the Halifax crash at Skipton-on-Swale, 5 August 1944; Mrs Helen Kirby; Mrs Connie McCoy; A. MacDonald; Bill Mitchener, 426 (Thunderbird) Squadron Association; Alan Micheson; Mrs Alice Metcalfe.; Ivan Mulley, Eastmoor Family Association; Archie Palmer, ex-51 Squadron; Stan Parker, 466/462 (RAAF) Squadrons Association; W. Noel Patterson, ex-158 Squadron; Rex Polendine, for permission to use his poems *Place of Ghosts* and *Concrete Cenotaph*; Ron Purcell, ex-640 Squadron for his account of the raid on Bochum; Group Captain P.W. Roser MBE and Flight Lieutenant D.M. Pleasant WRAF, RAF Leeming; Eddie Scott-Jones, ex-428 (Ghost) Squadron, RCAF; Chris. Sheehan, for the use of No.6 Group photographs; Brian Shields, Eastmoor Family Association; Jack Sherwin, 102 (Ceylon) Squadron Association; Harry Shinkfield, ex-77 Squadron; Harry Simister,MM, ex-158 Squadron; Peter Simpson,Dalton-on-Tees; Bill Smith, ex-158 Squadron; Colin Stokoe; Ron Stewart, 77 Squadron Association; David E. Thompson, for the loan of photographs and details of the Black Hambleton Halifax; Thorson's Publishing Group, for permission to use material from *Only Owls and Bloody Fools Fly at Night* (Kimber 1982); Ron Thurston, ex-158 Squadron, for permission to quote from *Baling out over Berlin*, which first appeared in *Intercom* (Aircrew Association) Autumn 1988; Colin Varley, ex-10 Squadron; Bill Williamson, ex-427 (Lion) Squadron; Jack Wingate, ex-10 Squadron; Geoff. Wood, Tholthorpe; Mrs and Mrs George Wood and daughter Georgina; Ted Wright; Those individuals and organisations who provided photographs.

Squadron Codes
No.4 Group RAF and No.6 (RCAF) Group,1939-45

The following codes relate to squadrons
commemorated by monuments in Yorkshire.

No.4 Group RAF

C8- 640 Sqdn
DY- 102(Ceylon)Sqdn
EY- 78 Sqdn
HL- 466 Sqdn RAAF
H7- 346(Guyenne)Sqdn
KN- 77 Sqdn
LK- 578 Sqdn
L8- 347(Tunisie)Sqdn
MH- 51 Sqdn
MP- 76 Sqdn
NP- 158 Sqdn
ZA- 10 Sqdn
Z5- 462 Sqdn RAAF

No.6(RCAF) Group

AL- 429(Bison)Sqdn
BM- 433(Porcupine)Sqdn
EQ- 408(Goose)Sqdn
KW- 425(Alouette)Sqdn
LQ- 405(Vancouver)Sqdn
NA- 428(Ghost)Sqdn
OW- 426(Thunderbird)Sqdn
PT- 420(Snowy Owl)Sqdn
QB- 424(Tiger)Sqdn
QO- 432(Leaside)Sqdn
SE- 431(Iroquois)Sqdn
WL- 434(Bluenose)Sqdn
VR- 419(Moose)Sqdn
ZL- 427(Lion)Sqdn

BEVERLEY

The 640 Squadron memorial which was erected 'in memory of those who did not come home' stands in the Memorial Garden, Beverley. Funded by Squadron Association members and brought to completion by Association Secretary Maurice Hepworth, it was unveiled by Squadron Leader H Coates DFC RAF(Ret'd) on Sunday 31 July, 1994, during a service of dedication led by Army Padre the Reverend John McNaughton and attended by some 150 former Squadron members and their wives. Cadets of 399 Squadron Air Training Corps mounted a Guard of Honour and a fly past was provided by a Sea King helicopter of 'E' Flight, 202(Search and Rescue)Squadron, Leconfield.

No.640 Squadron was formed at RAF Leconfield on 7 January, 1944 and remained there until it was disbanded on 7 May, 1945. The unit flew Halifax Mk IIIs for virtually the entire period of its operational

service, the Mk VI version being introduced to the Squadron in March 1945. The Squadron flew 2,442 sorties on 182 raids and lost forty-eight (2 per cent) aircraft. 347 aircrew failed to return from operations. Of these, 301 were classified 'Killed' or 'Missing'; forty-two became prisoners of war and four managed to evade capture. The names of those who lost their lives have been recorded in a Book of Remembrance located in St. Mary's Church, Beverley.

During No.640 Squadron's brief existence its flyers won the No.4 Group Bombing Trophy five times - a record unequalled by any other squadron in the Group. Sixty-four decorations were awarded to No.640 personnel: 59 DFCs; two bars to DFCs; two DFMs; and one BEM.

4/5 November 1944

Halifax Mk III MZ930/*C8-K* belonged to 640 Squadron, Leconfield.
On the night of 4/5 November, 1944, its crew was as follows: Dutchman Flying Officer Kees Goemans (pilot); Pilot Officer Ron Purcell (navigator); Pilot Officer 'Jock' Patterson (bomb aimer); Sergeant 'Paddy' Finnegan (flight engineer); Sergeant Freddie Nuttall (wireless operator); New Zealander Sergeant 'Kiwi' Korner (rear gunner); and Sergeant Ron Heath (mid-upper gunner). They were on their thirty-second operation and the last of their tour.

Their objective was Bochum, in the Ruhr. Bomber Command despatched 749 aircraft to the target and lost twenty-eight (3.7 per cent) of them. However, that was an average: some squadrons suffered greater losses. Among those which suffered the most was No.346 (Guyenne) Squadron, Elvington, which lost five (31.3 per cent) of the sixteen Halifaxes it sent. No.640 Squadron sent fifteen over the target and lost two (13 per cent). Nightfighters did most of the damage — but flak accounted for *K-King*.

Flak had been in evidence for some time during the approach to the target area, but it did not present a problem to the Leconfield crew until they turned for home. Jock Patterson had just released their bombs over the objective and Ron Purcell was busy setting a course for the return to base when they were caught. In a sky filled with anti-aircraft fire the gunners saw an extending line of flak bursts reaching out to cut across the flight path of the Halifax; they knew that it would cut them down and they shouted warnings to the pilot, but there was no time for him to take evasive action before one shell struck home close by the cockpit.

Halifax of No.640 Squadron, Leconfield. (via Maurice Hepworth)

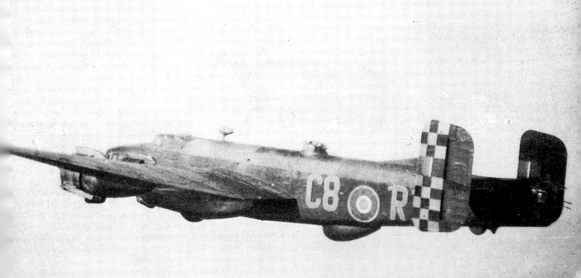

Ron Purcell remembers:

'My first awareness of the situation was a blinding flash and a loud explosion which started fires in several places in the front of the aircraft. Almost immediately, the body of our pilot, Kees Goemans, who had been killed instantly, came tumbling down the steps into the wireless operator and navigator compartments.'

Goemans fell on to the navigator, whose seat covered the forward escape hatch. When the pilot fell, his parachute deployed and the cords became entangled with the navigator and his seat, thus blocking access to the escape hatch.

The nose of the bomber dipped, and the Halifax began a slow spiral towards the earth.

Just before the shell hit, Freddie Nuttall was in the position he normally occupied on a bombing run — he was standing alongside the pilot and keeping an eye open for nightfighters. Miraculously, the shrapnel that killed Kees Goemans missed the wireless operator and it seems likely that Freddie Nuttall dragged his dead pilot from the cockpit

No.640 Squadron, Leconfield. (via Maurice Hepworth)

before scrambling into the Dutchman's seat and grappling with the controls. Although the wireless operator had not previously flown an aeroplane, he did achieve a measure of success: his efforts stopped the Halifax from spinning — but he did not arrest the dive.

While Freddie hung on to the controls in order to retain a measure of stability in the descent, Jock Patterson and Ron Purcell attempted to fight the fire and to clear the hatchway for their escape.

Purcell continues:

'Jock and I made strenuous efforts to clear the entanglement and attempted to beat out the flames, but because of the limited space and the difficulty of movement with the aircraft diving, we were not successful. Then, probably due to lack of oxygen, we both became unconscious.

'In what must have been a very short time afterwards, we suddenly both sat up at almost the same moment and we immediately made further efforts to beat out the flames. but it was absolutely futile: as each area of flames was extinguished

several more burst out elsewhere. When I tried to throw down the metal fire extinguisher I was using I found that it was red-hot and had stuck to my hands. It had to be torn off − taking most of the flesh off my hands with it.'

By that time three of the crew members had taken to parachutes. Rear gunner 'Kiwi' Korner simply rotated his turret and dropped out backwards into the night, seemingly without incident. The bale out by Ron Heath, mid-upper gunner, and flight engineer 'Paddy' Finnegan was more traumatic.

In spite of the crew's efforts to extinguish the flames, the fire continued to spread. When Finnegan went to the stowage area for his parachute, the compartment and its contents were burning. Not wishing to take the risk of baling out with a weakened parachute, he was given a piggy-back by Ron Heath. Unaccountably, they were not fastened to each other when they jumped; the flight engineer simply hung on to the mid-upper gunner as he leapt from the aircraft. When Heath's parachute opened, the sudden deceleration was too much for 'Paddy' Finnegan's grip and he fell some 10,000 feet to his death.

Meanwhile, Ron Purcell and Jock Patterson were still seeking to fight the fire. Then:

'Jock and I decided independently that it was time to abandon the aircraft and we headed for the back, to the other escape hatch. Jock was ahead and he beckoned me to follow. However, when I got to the stowing position for the parachutes, there were two in the rack still − and both were burning. I stamped out the flames of one and clamped it on my harness....As I was clamping on my 'chute I looked back to Freddie Nuttall, who was sitting in the pilot's seat and holding on to the controls to prevent the aircraft spinning. His flying suit was alight, but despite my shouting to him to come, he waved me to go to the rear escape hatch.

'When I reached the hatch, I sat on the edge. My trousers had been completely burnt off from the thighs down, and large areas of my legs were burnt. The skin had also been burnt off my hands and so I pushed one arm through the ring of the parachute and slid off into space.

'I have no recollection of actually pulling the ripcord, but the next moment the 'chute opened above me − and immediately burst into flames again.

'The descent to the ground was an eerie experience. Although there were flak bursts above me, I seemed to be floating in silence and I felt no actual sensation of pain. This was probably due to the intense cold and the obvious shock I was suffering, but I do remember seeing our burning aircraft dive and spin downwards. That must have been when Freddie Nuttall left the pilot's seat and released the controls. We learned later that Freddie's body was found in the aircraft, which crashed in the Rhine.'

Fifty years on, Ron Purcell has not forgotten Freddie Nuttall, an ultra-superstitious flyer who had his own ritualistic behaviours to keep himself and his colleagues safe in times of danger. The wireless operator, who always wore the same boots on operations and who always pulled a tuft of hair from under his flying helmet before take-off, regularly maintained that he had no idea what he was doing in such a hazardous job as aircrew.

'But despite this, he was always there when it was time for briefing. In fact, we didn't fly a single operation without him seated at his radio with his usual mournful expression and a little tuft of hair sticking out from under his helmet.'

On the night of 4/5 November, 1944, all of Freddie Nuttall's ritualistic behaviours failed him when he gave five others the chance of life at the cost of his own.

In Ron Purcell's words:

'He was a volunteer who wanted to do his bit in what he considered the best way possible; a man who, to the casual observer, was dead scared of flying (and probably was) but who went just the same — and when the moment of truth came, he was not found wanting.'

Such an epitaph could be applied to any of the 55,573 aircrew who lost their lives while serving with RAF Bomber Command during the Second World War.

Postscript:

'Jock' Patterson, 'Kiwi' Korner, Ron Heath and Ron Purcell landed safely and were made prisoners of war. Ron Purcell landed in the small garden of a house near Düsseldorf, where he was immediately picked up by an old man and a young boy who had seen the burning parachute settling earthwards and 'were under the impression I was a flare.' Those two fellows, together with a tearful old lady from the house, were very kind to him ('despite the fact that we had bombed the area the previous night') and they wrapped his hands, legs and face with paper bandages.

He was subsequently taken to a hospital at Gerrisheim, on the outskirts of Düsseldorf, where he underwent a number of skin-graft operations before being transferred to Stalag 17a Moosberg, near Munich. He was liberated from there by soldiers of Patton's 3rd Army on 29 April, 1945. When he eventually returned to England (on 10 May, 1945) he was informed by the medical officers who examined him that the grafting —

performed by German surgeons on an enemy — 'was some of the best
that they had seen...'

*Members of the crew of Halifax MZ930/C8-K, No.640 Squadron, Leconfield, shot down
over Bochum on the night of 4/5 November, 1944.* Left to right: *Sergeant Freddie Nuttall
(wireless operator); Sergeant Ron Purcell (navigator); Flying Officer Kees Goemans (pilot);
Sergeant Ron Heath (mid-upper gunner); and Sergeant 'Kiwi' Korner (rear gunner).*

(via Ron Purcell)

24 December 1944

No.640 Squadron Halifax Mk III *C8-X (Xray)* was one of 338 aircraft participating in a daylight attack on German airfields on 24 December 1944. Its crew consisted of Flying Officer Ron Buckland (pilot); Pilot Officer Craig Nightingale, RCAF (navigator); Pilot Officer Bill Holman, RCAF (bomb aimer); Pilot Officer Trevor Watkins (flight engineer); Sergeant 'Jock' Carr (wireless operator); Sergeant Bob Apps (mid-upper gunner); and Flight Sergeant Harry Stone (rear gunner). Their target was the nightfighter aerodrome at Essen/Mulheim.

Trevor Watkins remembers that:

'There was plenty of flak ahead on the run up to the target and there was a box barrage set at our height of about 20,000 feet. It treated all ranks alike but survival was a bit of a lottery, especially as we had to fly straight and level to drop the bombs and then fly straight some more to take a target photograph. I called up Bill, the bomb aimer, and gave him the £10 I owed him − just in case we got to be POWs.'

When Ron Buckland lined up the Halifax for its bombing run, Holman was all ready at the bomb sight in the nose of the aircraft. Then *X-Xray* was bracketed by anti-aircraft fire.

One shell exploded in front of the Halifax. Almost simultaneously, the bomb-aimer heard the flak burst and felt the Halifax being tossed by the accompanying shock-wave as a sherd of splintered steel tore a large hole in his windscreen and narrowly missed his head. The next burst to catch them followed almost immediately and exploded close by the starboard side. Its slamming impact damaged two engines and the tail plane − and shrapnel struck Ron Buckland on his right-hand side and flung him sideways like a toy.

Flight Engineer Trevor Watkins was waiting to open the bomb-doors when Buckland slumped forward and let go of the control column. Seconds later, the nose of the Halifax dipped earthwards. The Flight Engineer's subsequent report surely understates the drama of the moment:

'I opened the bomb-doors and then levelled out (the Halifax) before the skipper recovered sufficiently to hold the aircraft steady while we bombed.'

However, with the pilot unconscious, *X-Xray* was yawing around the sky quite dramatically but the decision was made to go on to their objective because that was considered safer than isolating themselves from the main group.

When Buckland recovered momentarily, he insisted on taking charge of the Halifax through the target area, but flying the aircraft at that time

Members of the crew of Halifax C8-X, No.640 Squadron, Leconfield, shot down over Essen/Mulheim 24 December, 1944. Left to right: *Sergeant 'Jock' Carr (wireless operator); Sergeant Jones (rear gunner)[position taken by Harry Stone on raid]; Sergeant Bob Apps (mid-upper gunner); Pilot Officer Trevor Watkins (flight engineer); Pilot Officer Bill Holman (bomb aimer); Flying Officer Ron Buckland (pilot); Pilot Officer Craig Nightingale (navigator).* (via Maurice Hepworth)

soon became a three-man effort: while the pilot endeavoured to fly the bomber between lapses of consciousness, Trevor Watkins supported him in his seat and navigator Craig Nightingale held the rudder bar steady. Their subsequent bombing photograph showed that they had coped sufficiently well to accurately deliver their bombs on the target.

Trevor Watkins continues:

'Once out of the target area, I asked the navigator to tell the skipper that we were over our lines. This he did and while Bill Holman held the control column I pulled the pilot out of his seat and took him to the rest position.'

Bomb aimer Bill Holman then assumed the role of temporary pilot — even though his previous flying experience was limited to a few hours on a Link Trainer — and mid-upper gunner Bob Apps stood in as temporary engineer while Trevor Watkins administered First Aid to his captain. It was then that the Flight Engineer realised how lucky his pilot (and, perhaps, all of them) had been.

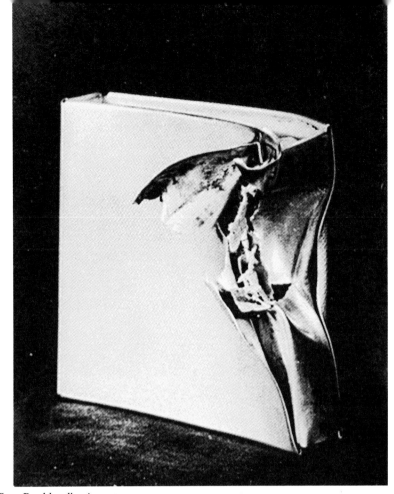

Ron Buckland's cigarette case. via Maurice Hepworth

> 'Ron had a packet of twenty cigarettes in his right-hand pocket and they were held in a strong metal case used by his father in the First World War. The case was up under his ribs and took the main force of the flak, but it was driven into his side.'

Thus a fortuitous occurence may well have saved the lives of both the pilot *and* his crew. Buckland's cigarette case had taken the brunt of the shrapnel's power and although the container had been savagely twisted and torn by the impact, it had offered its owner some protection from greater harm.

Although his cigarette case had taken most of the blow, Buckland was in great pain. However, he refused morphia and over the target he insisted on passing instructions to the bomb aimer. Subsequently, he began to shiver and to bleed from the mouth as a result of shock. When appeals were made for more clothing to keep the casualty warm, the rear gunner, Harry Stone, donated his own flying suit and returned to his turret in his shirt sleeves to endure the intense cold of a Halifax at 19,000 feet in December.

Although the bomb aimer's experience of flying was limited, it did turn out to be enough. However, when the bomber reached the English coast, Buckland insisted on taking control once again when they were given priority clearance at the emergency landing ground at Woodbridge, Suffolk.

Weak through loss of blood, Ron Buckland instructed his crew to bale out before he made his approach, but they refused. Wireless operator 'Jock' Carr later summed up the crew's feelings:

'We decided to stay because we had confidence in him. He justified that confidence by making a perfect landing, although he was so weak that his hand had to be put on the throttles.'

The 'perfect landing' was, in fact, a rather '...kangaroo affair...' but all crew members came through it unscathed. *X-Xray*, however, was sufficiently damaged by its encounter with flak to be written off. It was the *third* such loss the crew had experienced during their tour of duty.

Ron Buckland, Bill Holman and Trevor Watkins were each awarded the DFC (immediate) for their efforts that day; Harry Stone was subsequently awarded the DFM.

At the time of the Essen/Mulheim trip, the crew of *X-Xray* had flown some twenty operations, '...night and day, and of varying degrees of difficulty...' It took Ron Buckland two months to recover from his injuries. When he had done so, he and his crew went on to complete their tour of operations.

BUBWITH

The memorial to No.78 Squadron is located in the churchyard of All Saints, Bubwith, just one mile from the Squadron's wartime airfield of Brieghton. It takes the form of a rough hewn block of Cadby limestone inset with a crown metal plaque which bears the following inscription:

78 Squadron
4 Group Bomber Command
Yorkshire
1939 - 1945
To All Who Served

The outline of a Halifax bomber in relief is centrally placed below the inscription.

No.78 Squadron memorial at All Saints Church, Bubwith, close by Breighton aerodrome.

The fund that was to lead to the setting up of the Bubwith Memorial was started on 7 September, 1984, with an initial payment of £10 by a Preston doctor who was virtually a complete stranger to Squadron members.

No.78 Squadron's first biennial weekend reunion was held at the University of York on 7-8 September, 1984. During the course of the weekend, many of the 143 people who attended the reunion took the opportunity to revisit Breighton aerodrome, the Squadron's wartime home from June 1943 until the end of hostilities in Europe. Among those who visited the wartime base was Dr Derek Sayner, a general medical practitioner and aviation enthusiast, whose interest in Yorkshire wartime bomber squadrons had prompted him to contact the organizing secretary, Group Captain Ivor Easton, RAF (Ret'd), with a view to joining the reunion. It was at Breighton that Sayner suggested the idea of a memorial and gave Ivor Easton the first contribution. The idea was taken up that evening at the Reunion Dinner, when it was resolved that a memorial *should* be erected to all who had served with 78 Squadron during the Second World War and that the reunion committee would bring it to a result.

On Sunday, 7 September, 1986, with some 200 wartime members of the Squadron (including many from the Commonwealth and America) and their relatives in attendance, the memorial was unveiled by Sir Guy Lawrence DSO,OBE,DFC, Officer Commanding 78 Squadron in 1943-44, and the Dedication Service was conducted by the Bishop of Selby, the Right Reverend Clifford C. Barker MA, TD. The Chief Guest of Honour was Group Captain JB Tait DSO,DFC, Officer Commanding 78 Squadron in 1942. Other distinguished guests were Air Marshal Sir Leslie Mavor KCB,AFC,DL, Deputy Lord Lieutenant of North Yorkshire; Group Captain GH Rolfe CBE,ADC,RAF, Officer Commanding RAF Linton-on-Ouse; the Mayor and the Mayoress Borough of Boothferry, and other local dignitaries. The flypast was provided by a Wessex helicopter of 22 Squadron, trailing the RAF Ensign.

Since 1988 there has been a wooden plaque on the south side of the church which explains why the memorial is located in the churchyard. There is also a Visitors' Book for signing by ex-Squadron members and their close relatives.

When war broke out in September 1939, 78 Squadron was based at Dishforth and equipped with the Whitley MkI, the MkIVa, and the MkV. The MkI was dispensed with in December 1939 and the MkVa was dropped six months later, but the MkV remained in use with the Squadron until March 1942.

On 7 September, 1986, Sir Guy Lawrence DSO,OBE,DFC, Officer Commanding No.78 Squadron 1943-'44, unveiled the Bubwith Memorial. (Group Captain Ivor Easton)

The Squadron moved to Linton-on-Ouse on 13 December, 1939, but then returned to Dishforth during the following July and remained there until 7 April, 1941, when they took up a short term residence at Middleton-St-George before moving on to Croft on 20 October, 1941. They converted to the Halifax MkII during the following March before moving on yet again, first to Middleton-St-George (10 June, 1942) and then to Linton-on-Ouse (16 September, 1942), before settling at Breighton (16 June, 1943) for the remainder of the war years. Whilst at Breighton the squadron re-equipped with Halifax MkIII in June 1944 and then changed to MkIV version in the following April.

For the first ten months of the war No.78 was a reserve squadron, its role being to supplement the Group pool with trained crews, and it was not until the move back to Dishforth in July 1940, that it became operational. The first raid was carried out on the 19/20 of that month with the despatch of four Whitleys to Gelsenkirken. They returned safely, but on the following night the Squadron suffered its first loss

Breighton July 1992. Most of the site reverted to agricultural use but a local flying club occupies one corner of the old aerodrome.

when Whitley N1487 failed to return from Soest. It was the first of many. During the war years No.78 flew 6,237 sorties in 525 raids and lost 192 aircraft (3.1 per cent). The Squadron had the distinction of flying the most sorties in N0.4 Group – and having the third heaviest overall losses in Bomber Command.

8/9 July 1941

On the night of 8/9 July, 1941 forty-five Hampden bombers and twenty-eight Whitleys were despatched to attack the railway marshalling yards at Hamm. The raid cost the RAF seven aircraft – a loss rate of 9.6 per cent. No.78 Squadron (then based at Middleton-St-George) detailed twelve Whitley Mk Vs for the raid and lost four of them: Whitley Z6491, captained by Sergeant Jones, crash-landed near Thirsk on the return trip and Z6625 (Pilot Officer Wright) suffered a similiar fate near Sherbourne, Norfolk, both crews surviving; Whitley Z6555 (Sergeant OW McLean) is believed to have crashed in the North Sea and the fate of its crew is not known; the fourth loss, Whitley T4209/*EY-Q*, also ditched in the sea.

Whitley T4209/*EY-Q*, was crewed by Sergeant WM McQuitty; Pilot Officer EA Scott; Sergeant JF Haffenden; Sergeant D Clow; and Sergeant W Foster. Over the target they encountered heavy flak, which was sufficiently accurate to hole the perspex nose of their aircraft and to disable the starboard engine. En route for home they were attacked by a Me 110 night-fighter, but managed to escape relatively unscathed. They crossed the North Sea on one engine, losing height with the passing of each mile.

They were down to 400 feet of altitude when their luck ran out: eight miles from the Norfolk coast the remaining engine failed due to overheating. McQuitty successfully ditched the Whitley in the sea and the crew took to their dinghy. However, the rubber boat, perhaps damaged in the night-fighter attack, immediately became waterlogged and began to sink. Sergeant Haffenden, a strong swimmer, volunteered to strike out for the shore in search of help. It is estimated that he swam eight miles and then walked a further two miles before finding a Coast Guard Station and raising the alarm. Sad to say, his highly creditable effort was in vain: extensive searches of the area revealed no trace of the aircraft or its crew.

Superstition

'I was the pilot of a 78 Squadron Halifax crew from October 1942 to June 1943, and we developed our own particular method of ensuring our safe return.

'Our mid-upper gunner, 'Mac' MacQueen, was a young enthusiastic ex-ATC cadet who had

Whitley bombers over Cleveland circa 1941. Middleton-st-George aerodrome, known locally as Goosepool after a nearby farm, was opened officially in January 1941 as a station of No.4 Group, Bomber Command. It had a decoy aerodrome at Crathorne, some miles to the south east. In April 1941, sixteen Whitleys of No.78 Squadron arrived from Dishforth and that same month made raids on enemy shipping and against Berlin. In October of that year Croft was brought into use as a satellite airfield and that same month No.78 Squadron moved to Croft and began to convert to Halifax bombers. (Cleveland County Libraries, Redcar)

lied about his age and had joined the RAF for aircrew training at seventeen. He had just passed his eighteenth birthday when he joined the Squadron as a replacement for our original rear gunner who had got himself shot down with another crew. As a good luck present his girlfriend had sent him penguin mascot doll to carry with him on ops. It was adopted by the crew and promptly named Percy.

'Percy was further honoured by becoming our cockpit painting on the outside of the aircraft. He was depicted standing astride a large bomb, descending at about fifty degrees, holding two reins that ran down to a shark's mouth at the point. The mouth dripped blood and the blood drops became bombs as they reached the bottom line of the cockpit. One bomb was added each trip.

'In fact, that drawing became part of our take-off procedure as, taxiing out, I sang the first lines of the film theme from **Road to Morocco** *while patting the outside Percy on the bottom through the cockpit window. I had seen the film in London whilst on leave and it had been interrupted by a bomb dropping nearby, so consequently I could not remember all of it. But what I did remember, and always sang, was:*

> *We're off on the road to Morocco,*
> *It's better than the tunnel of love,*

Tell the boys that we won't be around,
Like Webster's Dictionary, we're Morocco bound.
This little ritual, and a check on the presence of Percy, were an essential part of our take-off
observance. And of course it worked — we all survived.'

Ron Read *Halifax pilot with 78 Squadron, October 1942 — June 1943*

Linton-on-Ouse, March 1943, Ron Read and his crew and ground crew standing in front of Halifax EY-C. **Left to right:** *Flight Sergeant R Lewis (wireless operator); Sergeant J McLean (air gunner); Pilot Officer V Freeman (navigator); Flight Lieutenant R Read (pilot); Flight Sergeant A Goodwin, Rhodesian Air Force (flight engineer); Pilot Officer H Laidlaw (bomb aimer). When this picture was taken they were one air gunner short.* (R Read)

'One night while on a return flight from Germany I had the unhappy experience of seeing no fewer than five aircraft shot down around us in the distance over a period of about an hour while we were running up to the Dutch coast on the way home. It was grimly fascinating to see in each case the short bursts of twinkling horizontal tracer — without any answering fire, unfortunately, so each must have been taken completely by surprise — followed by a small red fire, growing steadily into a larger ball. Then a slow curving fall to a final vertical plummet earthwards. Each time I wondered if the crew had managed to bale out safely, as we ourselves droned homewards, knowing full well that there were other nightfighters most probably stalking us too.'

Group Captain Tom Sawyer, Officer Commanding No.78 Squadron, Croft, 1941 in Only Owls and Bloody Fools Fly at Night Kimber 1982

Halifax MkII W1245/EY-B of No.78 Squadron, Middleton-St-George, was lost on the night of 11/12 August, 1942.

(IWM CH8034)

BURN

The memorial to No.578 Squadron is located in Burn Village (near Selby), alongside the A19 and opposite the *Wheatsheaf* public house. Funded by Association members and brought to fruition by Memorial Co-ordinator Eric Bowden, the monument was unveiled on 11 May, 1991, by the Association President, Wing Commander AGT James RAF (Ret'd), who commanded the Squadron during 1944-45. Some 250 people were in attendance and the dedication ceremony was conducted by the Reverend David Reynolds, Vicar of Brayton, and the Reverend Denys Terry, Burn's Methodist minister.

It had been intended that the unveiling ceremony would be carried out by ex-No.578 Squadron member Air Marshal Sir John Curtis, but he had to withdraw on the day before the ceremony was due to take place because of a family bereavement.

No.578 Squadron was formed at Snaith on 14 January, 1944, as part of 4 Group and was equipped with the Halifax Mk III. Three weeks later (on 6 February) it took up residence at Burn, which was to be home until 15 April, 1945, when the Squadron was disbanded.

The Squadron was in action within one week of its formation: on the night of 20/21 January, 1944, it carried out its first operation when five aircraft were despatched to Berlin.

During the course of their service with the Squadron, members were

awarded one VC, three DSOs, 143 DFCs and 82 DFMs. All of these were earned over an operational span of 155 raids and 2,721 sorties − at a cost of 72 aircraft (2.6 per cent) and 279 crew lost through death or capture.

One such aircraft was Halifax bomber LK797/*LK-E*, which was flown by Pilot Officer Cyril Barton and was lost on 31 March, 1944. 'Cy' Barton was awarded his posthumous Victoria Cross for 'unsurpassed courage and devotion to duty' on the Nuremberg operation that was to cost him his life.

No.578 Squadron Memorial, Burn, nr Selby.

Pilot Officer Cyril Barton, VC. (via Alan Micheson)

30/31 March 1944

On the night of 30/31 March, 1944, Bomber Command sent 795 aircraft to attack Nuremberg and lost ninety-five (11.9 percent) of them; a further seventy-one were damaged, eleven so badly that they were beyond repair. A total of 545 aircrew were killed, 155 became prisoners of war, and twenty-six returned to base injured. It was the biggest single loss to be suffered by Bomber Command in any raid during the Second World War.

No.578 Squadron, Burn, contributed twelve Halifaxes to the operation. One of them was Halifax Mk III LK797/*LK-E*, piloted by Pilot Officer Cyril Barton. His crew consisted of Flying Officer W Crate (bomb- aimer); Sergeant J Kay (wireless operator); Sergeant L Lambert (navigator); Sergeant M Trousdale (flight-engineer); Sergeant F Brice (rear-gunner); and Sergeant HD Wood (mid-upper gunner). It was their eighteenth operation.

German nightfighters were very active that night and they accounted for most of the losses on the Nuremberg trip: Barton's crew encountered two of them. Some seventy miles from the target *LK-E* was intercepted by a Ju 88 nightfighter, which was joined in the ensuing battle by a Me 210. When the engagement was over the bomber's starboard inner engine had been badly damaged, the fuel system had been holed, the radio and navigational aids had been destroyed, and the intercom links had been cut.

In the confusion that followed, Crate, Kay and Lambert believed that the order to bale out had been given and they took to their parachutes. Disregarding the condition of his aircraft and the absence of three crew members, Barton pressed on to his target and bombed what he thought was Nuremberg, though it was, in fact, Schweinfurt. Shortly afterwards, the propeller of the damaged starboard inner engine flew off.

In spite of these difficulties, the crew opted to attempt to return to England, Barton navigating by the stars and aided by a compass. Perhaps against the odds, they reached the continental coast without interception.

Over the sea and in darkness, with the navigator gone and the navigational aids destroyed in the attack, Barton was by no means sure of his geographical position. Thus, when it was suggested that they could well be farther to the south than anticipated and were, perhaps, flying *down* the Channel (and towards the Atlantic) rather than across it, Barton decided to alter course to a more northerly heading.

They continued flying northwards until, in dawn's early light, they made landfall near Sunderland, some ninety miles north of their base:

Cyril Barton and his crew photographed at Brieghton, 1943. Back (L-R): *Sergeant J Kay (wireless operator); Flying Officer W Crate (bomb aimer); Pilot Officer Cyril Barton (pilot); Sergeant Len Lambert (navigator); Sergeant Maurice Trousdale (flight engineer).*
Front (L-R): *Sergeant Fred Brice (rear gunner); Sergeant 'Timber' Wood (mid-upper gunner).*

(via A Micheson)

safety was within reach – or so it seemed. However, their IFF (Identification Friend or Foe)* was not functioning and as they approached the coast of County Durham they were fired upon by anti-aircraft defences whose operators assumed that the Halifax was a German raider.

Eye-witness Alan Micheson, who was then twelve years old and living in Hewitt Avenue, Ryhope, had just returned to bed at the end of an air raid *Alert* when:

'I heard the sound of an aircraft coming in from the sea. The anti-aircraft artillery at the top of our street started firing two or three rounds. Looking out of my bedroom window, I watched the plane heading towards the colliery from the direction of Hendon Docks. The aircraft turned round the stone-heap and made out to sea again.

About ten minutes later it returned, a light flashing from its nose, and the artillery fire ceased. This time however, the aircraft sounded different, as though in difficulties. It was much lower and its port and starboard navigation lights were on as it passed over

(*) All British aircraft were equipped with an IFF (Identification – Friend or Foe) transmitting device which was operated when within British radar range. When activated, it gave a distinctive periodic elongation to the blip produced on a radar screen by an approaching aircraft and thus enabled defenders to distinguish friendly aircraft from hostile.

*The wreckage of Cyril Barton's Halifax LK797LK-E in the yards at Ryhope Colliery, 31 March, 1944. The young boy to the left of the group of onlookers is Alan Micheson, who was responsible for the erection of the plaque on the Ryhope War Memorial in November 1985. (*Imperial War Museum HU4021*)*

our rooftop by no more than fifty feet. I ran from my room across the landing into my parents' room and watched in horror as it fell on the colliery, by the gangway.'

The artillery barrage had forced Barton to turn out to sea again until Sergeant Wood could connect up an Aldis lamp to signal the SOS which would persuade the defenders to cease firing. However, that extra flying time had virtually exhausted what meagre fuel remained in the tanks. The port engines stopped as the Halifax crossed the coast for the second time and, with only one engine still working, the bomber dipped earthwards.

The crew had only just enough time to follow their captain's instructions to assume crash positions before the bomber grounded at Hollycarrside. It clipped the end of a row of miners' houses in West Terrace, demolishing one and slightly damaging another. The Halifax then separated into several parts as it careered into the yard of Ryhope colliery, where flying debris killed one miner and injured another.

Sergeant Wood and Sergeant Brice survived the crash virtually unscathed. Sergeant Trousdale also survived, though he suffered injuries which put him on the danger list for several days. But Cyril Barton's condition was far more serious: he was mortally injured and died thirty minutes after the crash. He was twenty-two years old.

On 27 June, 1944, Cyril Barton was posthumously awarded the Victoria Cross in recognition of his 'unsurpassed courage and devotion to duty'. Sergeants Wood, Brice and Trousdale were each awarded the Distinguished Flying Medal.

Halifax *LK-E* was one of three aircraft (25 percent) lost on that raid by No.578 Squadron. With the wisdom of hindsight, it can be said that if Barton had held his original course over the sea he might well have made a safe return — for when he changed direction to a more northerly heading he was a mere twenty minutes from the emergency landing ground at Woodbridge (near Ipswich).

Alan Micheson was twelve years old when he witnessed the crash of Barton's Halifax. With the passing of the years he found himself wondering why it was that there had been no recognition anywhere in Ryhope '...of an event which had culminated in the award of the country's highest award for gallantry...' However, it was not until he was posted to RAF Leeming as a National Serviceman that he became deeply involved in researching the circumstances leading to Cyril Barton's demise.

With his growing admiration for the ways in which the twenty-two year old bomber-pilot had coped with the Nuremberg incident and the later consequences it imposed upon the crew of *LK-E*, Micheson's research turned into a crusade c.1978, when he resolved to get Ryhope to give public recognition to the pilot. As the campaigner was later to proclaim:

> 'What we have to remember, but unfortunately has been too easily forgotten here and for far too long, is the sacrifice that this young airman made... Because of his unselfish actions, many lives were saved that morning. For not only did he steer his badly stricken bomber away from the houses below him, but also from the screens of the colliery, where many men were working and who were directly in his flight path. Let us also not forget the harrowing experience which he had endured only five hours earlier over Nuremberg.'

Four-and-a-half years of campaigning against Sunderland Council Planning Committee eventually brought the promise of a memorial on site and assurance was given that '...a large piece of rock from Otterburn would be transported to the site of the crash, and a suitable inscription mounted on it...' But shortly afterwards the Council reneged on the idea and the plan was scrapped.

Alan then enlisted the support of Gordon Bagier MP, who was subsequently informed in a letter (March 1985) from the then Chief Executive of the Borough of Sunderland that '...I have some sympathy with the correspondent, but the view is strongly taken that *he* (Barton) *has no direct connection with this area* and therefore I can see no immediate prospect of any recognition of him...'

Alan Micheson's one-man battle to gain recognition for Cyril Barton took a significant step forward when the *Sunderland Echo* took up the cause and printed the letter. Its publication provoked a storm of protest and instigated a surge of local support in the 'Letters to Editor column' over a five-week period, from ex-servicemen and the general public alike. One writer expressed the issue succintly enough:

> 'To say that there can be no prospect of recognition of his (Barton's) valour because he had no direct connection with the area appears to me to be a distasteful piece of blinkered parochialism. Cyril Barton and thousands like him flew, fought and died not only for the people of their home towns but for the liberty of every one of us...'

Additional support came from the chairman of the Ryhope Workingmen's Club, who invited the formation of a local committee to pressure the Council's decision and, if necessary, to organize a public appeal to finance a memorial because:

> '...I actually entered the aircraft after the crash to try and help, but was immediately told to get out as it was likely to explode. Perhaps I may be able to help now...'

Given the scale of the protest, Sunderland Council finally relented. A commemorative plaque was subsequently attached to the Ryhope War Memorial and it was unveiled on Remembrance Sunday, 10 November, 1985, by Cyril Barton's sisters, Joyce Voysey and Cynthia Maidment, in the presence of the surviving few members of *LK-E*: Freddie Brice, 'Timber' Wood and Len Lambert.

The RAF was represented by Group Captain Bill Sweatman, Officer Commanding RAF Fylingdales, and Wing Commander Keith Walters, Chief Flying Instructor, RAF Church Fenton. The occasion provided the opportunity for the survivors of the crash to renew old contacts with citizens of Ryhope who had gone to their aid so many years before: Les Lawther, who had pulled three from the wreck; Harry Hicks, the ambulance driver who had ferried them to Cherry Knowle Hospital; and nursing sisters Eva Sparks and Celia Herbert who had cared for the survivors during their time there.

It was an occasion much appreciated by 'Timber' Wood:

'I was very proud to be present at Ryhope last Sunday to see so many present at St Paul's Church and also at the memorial when my pilot Cyril Joe Barton VC was honoured by the community. I know he too would have been delighted.'

The day was no less memorable for Freddie Bryce:

'For me to have reason to return after 41 years, to meet people who helped us on that fateful morning... just to be able to say a humble thank you and shake their hand... is something I shall never forget...'

The thoughts of Alan Micheson on that day are not recorded but he must have felt intense pleasure at bringing his campaign to a most satisfying conclusion. Freddie Bryce voiced the thoughts of many when he stated:

'...At the end of the day, my thanks must go to Alan Micheson, who after a long campaign, eventually reached his goal, the burning ambition of the twelve year old lad who saw us crash.'

Perhaps it is worth considering that in achieving his objective, Alan showed a measure of tenacity and strength of purpose that Cyril Barton would have most surely have appreciated.

The Barton Plaque is attached to the base of the War Memorial that stands on Ryhope green. The inscription reads as follows:

To the memory of Pilot Officer Cyril Joe Barton VC (168669) RAFVR. No.578 Squadron who died on the 31st March 144, after crash-landing his crippled Halifax bomber south-west of Hollycarrside, thus avoiding Ryhope. He displayed unsurpassed courage and devotion to duty, then sacrificed his life to save others and was posthumously awarded the Victoria Cross.

10 November, 1985. Alan Micheson with Cyril Barton's sisters, Joyce Voysey (left) and Cynthia Maidment, both of whom unveiled the Ryhope plaque. (A. Micheson)

Not all the dangers came from the enemy. Flying Officer Bob Davies and the crew of Halifax Mk III MZ559/LK-F (578 Squadron, Burn) had a lucky escape during an attack on Venlo (Holland) airfield on 3 September, 1944, when a bomb from a higher flying Lancaster plunged through the fuselage before striking the aerodrome. In spite of the damage, the Halifax behaved normally and the crew made a safe return to England and landed at the American airfield at Old Buckenham. (L to R): Bob Burn (navigator); Sam Brown (rear gunner); Bob Davies (pilot); Wally Scarth (flight engineer); Charlie Hayward (mid upper gunner); Vernon Corbett (bomb aimer); Dick Tither (wireless operator)

On 18 November, 1944, while being flown by another crew, MZ559 was returning from operations against Munster and was in the landing circuit when it was in collision with Halifax NR241/MH-A of 51 Squadron, Snaith. There were no survivors from either crew.

(Bob Davies via David E. Thompson)

The crew of Halifax Mk III LK830/LK-0 (578 Squadron, Burn) line up in front of their aircraft. (L to R) : Flight Sergeant Chuck Adams (rear gunner); Sergeant Pete Romback (mid-upper gunner); Pilot Officer Bob Majaki (bomb aimer); Pilot Officer Jim Bluring (pilot); Flight Sergeant George Costidell (wireless operator); Sergeant K Shearsby (flight engineer); Flight Officer 'Mac' MacNaughton (navigator); two squadron wireless operators.

They went to Bochum on the night of 9/10 October, 1944. On the homeward journey their aircraft was fired upon by an unidentified Halifax flying ahead of them. Ken Shearsby was wounded in three places; Bob Majaki was killed instantly. Such an encounter would be bad at any time — but the fact that the Bochum operation was the crew's fortieth (and final) trip of a tour gave Majaki's death added poignancy. (via Chuck Adams)

The pre-operation ritual of Maurice Clark and his crew, No.578 Squadron, Burn.

(via Chuck Adams)

DRIFFIELD

The memorial stone to No.462 and No.466 Squadrons RAAF stands in the Memorial Gardens, Driffield, and consists of a slab of polished Australian diorite granite. It bears the following inscription below the Squadrons' badge, which is flanked by a Wellington bomber and Halifax bomber in outline:

In honour of those who made
the supreme sacrifice
and the men and women who
served with 462 and 466 RAAF
Squadrons of Bomber Command
Middle East, Driffield and Leconfield
1942 – 1945
Dedicated 12-9-93   Lest We Forget

The stone was unveiled on Sunday, 12 September, 1993, during a service of dedication and remembrance which was led by local religious leaders from three denominations and which was attended by some two hundred and fifty veterans and a large number of the general public. Dignitaries in attendance included the Earl and Countess of Halifax, the High Sheriff of Humberside, and past and present civic leaders of Driffield. The Australian Air Defence Staff in the United Kingdom was represented by Wing Commander Brian Lane and Squadron Leader David Richardson.

Prior to the service, the Driffield Silver Band and fourteen standard bearers headed a parade of some two hundred and fifty veterans to the site. The marchers included fifty ex-aircrew who had returned from Australia for the occasion.

The unveiling was performed jointly by Group Captain RH Waterhouse, CBE DFC AFC Silver Star(USA) (RAF Ret'd), who was the station commander at Leconfield 1944, and by Wing Commander RE Bailey OBE DSO DFC (RAAF Ret'd), who commanded No.466 Squadron in 1944. The flypast was provided by a Sea King helicopter of No.202 Squadron, Leconfield, trailing the Australian national flag.

The following morning, Bruce Otton, President of the No.466/462 (RAAF) Squadrons' Association, together with a group of members, visited the children of the five local schools to present the units' plaque and to charge them with care of the memorial for future years.

No.466 Squadron, Royal Australian Air Force (RAAF), was formed at Driffield on 15 October, 1942, and was initially equipped with the Wellington Mk II, but this was changed to the Mk X version during the following month. The Australians re-located to Leconfield on 2 December, 1942, when moves commenced to adapt Driffield for use by heavy bombers and preparations were made to lay down concrete runways. No.466 Squadron's own conversion to four-engined 'heavies' occurred in late 1943, when they were allocated Halifax Mk IIs in September of that year. However, the association was short-lived: they took possession of Halifax Mk IIIs two months later and operated the type until the end of the war in Europe. No.466 returned to Driffield when the base had been adapted to its role as a heavy bomber station; they arrived on 3 June, 1944, and stayed until the cessation of hostilities.

During its wartime service No.466 Squadron RAAF carried out 3,328 sorties in 264 raids, at a cost of 352 personnel killed. Squadron Association figures claim that seventy-three aircraft were lost on operations with a further twenty-three being lost due to crashes in this country.[1]

No.462 Squadron RAAF operated Halifax Mk IIs for the first two years of its existence after being formed at Fayid (Egypt) in September 1942. It was disbanded in February 1944, while en-route to Celone (Italy), and was re-numbered No.614 Squadron. It was reformed at Driffield six months later and was equipped with Halifax Mk IIIs. The Squadron spent only four months at the East Yorkshire base. In December 1944 it was transferred to No.100 Group, Foulsham (Norfolk) to be employed in Radio Counter Measure duties.

During its wartime service, the Squadron lost thirty-seven aircraft and 124 personnel killed. These figures include twenty aircraft and fifty-six personnel (of which twenty-six were ground crew) lost in the Middle East. Losses from Driffield accounted for seven aircraft and fifteen crewmen killed; the toll incurred at Foulsham amounted to ten aircraft and fifty-three killed.[2]

All personnel lost by both squadrons during the 1939-45 conflict are listed in the Book of Remembrance in St Mary's Parish Church, Beverley.

---

1. With the exception of the 'raids' figure which is taken from *Bomber Command War Diaries* (1990 ed) p773 these details were provided by Stan Parker, No.462-466 Squadron Association. *Bomber Command War Diaries* confirms the number of sorties but lists only 65 aircraft lost.

2. Stan Parker, No.462-466 Squadron Association. *Bomber Command War Diaries* (1990 ed) p772, gives only the figures for UK service and lists Driffield's record as 54 sorties in 45 raids at a cost of 6 aircraft lost; Foulsham's figures are given as 621 sorties in 63 RCM operations at a cost of 7 aircraft lost.

Wing Commander RE Bailey OBE DSO DFC RAAF Ret'd (centre) and Group Captain RH Waterhouse CBE DFC AFC Silver Star (USA) RAF Ret'd (right)who unveiled the Driffield memorial to No.462/466 Squadrons RAAF on 12 September, 1993, (Hull Daily Mail)

4/5 November, 1944

No.466 (RAAF) Squadron contributed sixteen Mk III Halifaxes to the total force of 749 aircraft which Bomber Command launched against Bochum in the early evening of 4 November, 1944. Total losses amounted to twenty-eight aircraft (3.7 per cent), to which No.346 (Guyenne) Squadron, Elvington, contributed five (31.3 per cent) of the sixteen it despatched.

No.466 (RAAF) Squadron had one 'early returner' and lost two (13.3 per cent) of the remaining fifteen Halifaxes which pressed on to the target. One of those failing to return was NR132/*HD-Z* (Flight Sergeant NCR Dodgson). The other was LV936/*HD-D*, crewed by Flight Lieutenant Joe B. Herman (pilot); Flying Officer David Underwood (bomb aimer); Flight Sergeant J Vivash mid-upper gunner); and Flight Sergeant M 'Mac' Wilson (rear gunner).

Perhaps the trip got off to a bad start for Herman and his crew when they witnessed the collision of two aircraft − and the potential loss of fourteen lives − just as they were approaching the Dutch coast, but their evening was destined to get worse.

They were coned for the first time that night as they crossed Germany en route to the target, but they managed to escape to darkness without any damage being inflicted. It was then that Herman ordered his crew to put on their parachutes − perhaps because of a premonition he might have had. However, he neglected to follow his own instruction: as he steered his aircraft towards Bochum *his* parachute remained stored in the flight engineer's compartment. Over the target they were coned a second time and were engaged by heavy flak, but again they escaped unscathed. However, their luck failed them 17,000 ft over Bochum, when they were caught by anti-aircraft fire just after they had dropped their bombs and were leaving the target area.

The first burst caused fire to break out just behind the main spar. While Knott was attempting to extinguish the flames, the bomber took further hits which wounded Vivash in his right leg, punctured the fuel tanks in the port and starboard wings and started a blaze that threatened to engulf all. With Knott still attempting to forstall the inevitable, Herman ordered the crew to bale out. Duncan, Underwood and Nicholson exited through the forward escape hatch, while Wilson left via the rear turret. Vivash and Knott were still on board when Herman reached for his own parachute − just as the blazing starboard wing broke up and the bomber snapped into a spin. Seconds later, the fuel tanks exploded, the Halifax disintegrated and Joe Herman and his crew-mates were catapulted into the night. Unlike Vivash and Knott, Joe Herman had no parachute with him. He fell towards the earth surrounded by the debris of his aircraft and making attempts to grab at any pieces of wreckage that might be the 'chute he had left behind. All efforts were to no avail. He estimates that he had fallen some 12,000ft before he collided with the object that was to save his life: he grabbed it instinctively and held on for dear life. Miraculously, the 'object' turned out to be the legs of Vivash, the mid-upper gunner, whose parachute had just started to deploy. They came down to earth together, and though their landing was understandably heavy, and broke two of Joe Herman's ribs, both survived their ordeal and spent three days 'on the run' before being captured. They spent the rest of the war as POWs, as did Harry Knott.

Strange as it may seem, the three who might have been expected not to survive, did so: the four who baled out before their aircraft exploded, did not live to tell the tale. Why that should be so remains a mystery. Geoffrey Jones points out that:

> 'What happened to the rest is not known. The four of them who baled out before the Halifax disintegrated were buried four days after the raid at a place named Neviges, 15 miles south-west of Bochum. After the war they were re-interred at Cleves War Cemetery.' (*Raider: the Halifax and its Flyers*, Kimber 1978 p223).

The cause of their death is unknown, but 462/466 Association member Stan Parker believes that Nicholson, Duncan, Underwood and Wilson were taken prisoner and killed by their captors whilst in transit to a POW camp.

*Halifax MkIII No.LV833 was delivered to No.466 (RAAF) Squadron, Leconfield, in January 1944. The aircraft was operational for six months before failing to return from Stuttgart in July 1944 (*RAF Museum, *5994-10)*

5 March, 1944

The raid on Chemnitz on the night of 5/6 March, 1945, cost Bomber Command thirty-one (4.1 per cent) of the 760 bombers scheduled to take part in the attack. Nine of the aircraft lost belonged to No.6(RCAF) Group, but they did not succumb to flak or to nightfighters: they fell victim to severe icing as they climbed away from their Yorkshire bases and crashed before they had even cleared the county boundary.

A No.4 Group Halifax of No.466 (RAAF) Squadron also encountered icing shortly after taking off from its base — and although the consequences were not as calamitous as those experienced by Canadian crews the consequence was not without tragedy.

When Australian Flying Officer Ron Swain and his crew took off from Driffield at 17.00 hrs the cloud base was down to 400 ft and there were warnings of icing conditions en route to the target. Normally they flew in Halifax Mk III NR250/*HL-N*, but the previous evening *N-Nan* had been a victim of Operation 'Gisela' while being flown by another crew and had been shot down (the crew baled out over Waddington; *N-Nan* flew on to crash at Friskney, near Skegness). Swain's replacement for the Chemnitz trip was Halifax Mk III LV949/*HL-W*. Heavy with fuel and a full bomb load, the Halifax commenced its ascent in 10/10ths cloud that reached up to 8,000ft, but progress was slow: *W-Willie* did not have the power of its predecessor. Complications associated with the prevailing weather added to the difficulty.

The ice came sooner than crews might have been led to expect at briefing: the Halifax was still in the Driffield area and had reached 5,000ft when ice started to cocoon the control surfaces. The problem intensified with every increase in altitude, but the aircraft managed to claw through a further 3,000ft of ice-bearing cloud before Swain began to experience difficulty in forcing his aircraft higher. By then, severe icing was jamming the controls and making the Halifax unmanageable: the pilot warned his crew to be ready to bale out.

The Halifax was at 8,000ft and had just broken free of cloud when it began to stall. Then it was falling and Swain was shouting to his crew to 'Jump! Jump as quick as you can!' while he attempted to pull his aircraft out of what seemed to be an uncontrollable dive.

Most of the crew evacuated without difficulty, but two members had delayed exits. Rear gunner Frank Bristow turned his turret through ninety degrees and, with one hand clutching the handle of his parachute, he flipped backwards into the night. However, he did not travel far because his left foot jammed on an unseen obstacle in the turret and held him: instead of falling clear he found himself trailing behind the Halifax as it plummeted to earth. He remembers that when all efforts

The crew of Halifax HL-W *(466 (RAAF) Squadron, Driffield) who found themselves in difficulties on 5 March, 1945.* L-R (back row): *Flight Sergeant Fred Ray (wireless operator); Sergeant Frank Bristow RAF (rear gunner); Sergeant Geoff Bocking RAF (mid-upper gunner); Flight Sergeant Ted Gates (flight engineer).* L-R (front row): *Flight Sergeant Reg Roff RAF (bomb aimer); Flying Officer Ron Swain (pilot); Flight Sergeant Brian Harrison (navigator).* (Frank Bristow via David E. Thompson)

to free himself failed he tried to get back into the turret, but there was no way that he could combat the power of the buffeting slipstream. His position seemed hopeless — then he remembered his parachute.

That night Frank Bristow was *twice* saved by his parachute. He was still snared when he pulled the rip-cord and heard the terrific crack as the canopy deployed. He heard it at the same time as the metal retaining hooks on his harness struck him forcibly below both eyes and knocked him out. When he came to he was without his left boot but he was descending through cloud and supported by a canopy of silk: the opening of the 'chute had wrenched him free.

He landed in a field — to be met by two young boys who asked if they could '...carry your parachute, mister?' A passing motorist gave him a lift to Driffield, where he anxiously awaited news of his crewmates.

As the night wore on he learned that all of the crew apart from the pilot had baled out, but Fred Ray was missing. The wireless operator had been the last to go, Ron Swain insisting that Fred bale out while he (the pilot) tried to get the aircraft stable and before it was too late.

Such is the nature of luck that shortly after the wireless operator evacuated the aircraft, Ron Swain recovered control of the bomber and eventually landed it at the emergency landing strip at Carnaby. Ray, however, was cruelly served. No one knows whether he survived his bale out because it subsequently transpired that he had landed in Bridlington Bay, some distance from the shore. His body was washed up at Hornsea six weeks later. He was twenty-two years old.

Superstition

'When we crewed up at Kinloss in 1944 a kind family called McIntosh invited us to Sunday lunch and gave each member a McIntosh scarf. We wore them on every flight. My bomb aimer also wore his baby's bootees on his tunic. We would not take off without our scarves.'

[Mike Cranfield, pilot, ex-No.77 Squadron]

The 'Black Thursday' Memorial, Driffield aerodrome

DRIFFIELD

On 'Black Thursday', 15 August, 1940, the Battle of Britain was at its height. Believing that available RAF fighter squadrons were heavily committed in the south, Luftwaffe bombers launched two almost simultaneous large-scale attacks in daylight against aerodromes in the north of England.

Sixty-three Heinkel 111s of KG26 (Stavanger, Norway), escorted by twenty-one Messerschmitt 110s, had the airfields of Dishforth and Linton-on-Ouse as their primary targets, with Newcastle, Sunderland and Middlesbrough as secondary aiming points. Further south, some thirty Junkers 88s of KG30 (Aalborg, Denmark) struck at Driffield aerodrome.

The Ju.88s were intercepted off Flamborough Head by Spitfires of 616 Squadron (Leconfield) and Hurricanes of 73 Squadron (Church Fenton) and lost several of their number before reaching their target. The remainder, however, successfully pressed home their attack, during the course of which 169 bombs of various calibres were dropped and the airfield strafed with machine-gun fire.

As a consequence, ten RAF Whitley bombers were destroyed, and four aircraft hangars were considerably damaged. Thirteen airfield personnel (including one civilian employee) were killed and a further fourteen hospitalized.

The defenders claimed nine enemy aircraft shot down during the Driffield raid. Most fell into the sea, but two crashed on land in the Bridlington area.

The tablet that commemorates the raid was erected by the Driffield Branch of the Royal Air Force Association, supported by the Town Council. It was unveiled by the Mayoress of Driffield, Mrs Brenda Pinkney, on 18 August, 1990, in a ceremony attended by some 250 people. Among those present were representatives of No.102 and No.77 Squadrons and the East Yorkshire Regiment, all of whom lost personnel in the raid.

The old aerodrome is now the Alamein Barracks of the Army School of Mechanical Transport. The memorial is sited just inside the main gate and in front of the former Station HQ.

ELVINGTON

When war broke out in September 1939 No.77 Squadron was operating from Driffield. It moved to Linton-on-Ouse in August 1940 but stayed only two months before moving further north, to Topcliffe. On 5 September, 1941, it transferred to Leeming for an eight-month stay, after which it was seconded to Coastal Command (Chivenor) until October 1942. The Squadron took up residence at the newly-completed airfield at Elvington on 5 October, 1942, and remained there until May 1944. It made its final move of the war years in the middle of that month when it re-located to Full Sutton.

Already equipped with Whitley IIIs before the outbreak of hostilities, the Squadron changed to the Mark V version in September 1939 and retained this until the move to Elvington, when the Whitleys were traded in for Halifax Mk IIs. These were replaced by Halifax Mk Vs in April 1944. The move to Full Sutton coincided with a further change of aircraft − to the Halifax Mk III − and the Squadron continued to operate this type until March 1945, when the Mk VI was assigned to the unit.

The Squadron took part in 486 operations and carried out 5,379 sorties, during the course of which it lost 131 aircraft (2.4 percent) and some 900 personnel.

The No.77 Squadron Association was formed in 1988 and at its first meeting the question of raising a suitable memorial was discussed. Wing Commander 'Bobby' Sage, the Chairman of the Association and President of the Yorkshire Air Museum, had been offered a rose-marble column and this was subsequently incorporated

No.77 Squadron Memorial at Elvington aerodrome, which now forms part of the Yorkshire Air Museum.

into a design submitted by the Association Secretary, Ron Stewart.

The memorial was dedicated on Saturday, 16 September, 1989, during a service attended by some 200 people and led by the Reverend Donald Tittley, an ex-77 Squadron rear gunner who was shot down over Magdeburg in January 1944. It stands just inside the main gate of the old aerodrome, at what is now the Yorkshire Air Museum, Elvington.

The control tower at Elvington aerodrome, now the home of the Yorkshire Air Museum.

23/24 August, 1943

During the period August 1943 – March 1944, Bomber Command carried out nineteen major raids on the German capital, in what has since become known as the 'Battle of Berlin'. When it was over, bomber crews had flown 10,813 sorties against the 'Big City' and had lost 625 (5.8 per cent) aircraft: 2,690 aircrew had paid the ultimate price; a further 987 had been made prisoners of war and an additional fifty-two had managed to evade capture and, with the help of brave men and women in Occupied Europe, would eventually return safely to England.[1]

No.4 Group RAF took part in nine of the attacks. In total, the Group mounted 1,183 sorties against Berlin during that phase of the air war and lost 106 (8.9 per cent) aircraft and 717 personnel (487 of whom were killed).[2]

No.77 Squadron, Elvington, participated in seven of the raids and flew 134 sorties. Sixteen (11.9 per cent) aircraft were lost as a consequence; ninety-six aircrew lost their lives and twenty-one became prisoners of war.

The crew of No.77 Squadron Halifax JD379/KN-M pose with their ground crew.
Back row (L-R): *3rd Pilot Officer Philip Stiff (wireless operator); 5th Sergeant Alan Pears (bomb aimer); 6th Flying Officer Charlie Rollings (rear gunner).*
Front row (L-R): *3rd Flight Sergeant Bill Plunkett (navigator); 4th Sergeant Charlie Brister (mid-upper gunner); 5th Flight Sergeant Alex Massie (pilot); 7th Sergeant Reg Croft (flight engineer).* (C Brister)

1. Middlebrook (1988)
2. No.6 (RCAF) Group crews flew 1,220 sorties against the German capital during that phase of the air war and lost a total of 91 (7.5 percent) aircraft and 573 personnel (437 of whom were killed); (op cit)

A Halifax Mk II (coded KN-X) *of No.77 Squadron, Elvington, makes a low pass over the aerodrome* (IWM CH 10594)

Elvington-based Halifax JD379/*KN-M* was one of the 727 aircraft that raided Berlin on the night of 23/24 August, 1943. Its crew consisted of: Flight Sergeant Alex Massie (pilot); Flight Sergeant Bill Plunkett (navigator); Sergeant Alan Pears (bomb aimer); Sergeant Reg Croft (flight engineer); Pilot Officer Philip Stiff (wireless operator); Sergeant Charlie Brister (mid-upper gunner); and Flying Officer Charlie Rollings (rear gunner).

The attack cost Bomber Command fifty-six (7.9 per cent) aircraft lost and a further forty-five (6.2 per cent) damaged. It is believed that the 'moderately intensive' flak which was encountered en route was responsible for twelve of the losses, six of them in the target area. However, the main toll was exacted by nightfighters. Zero hour for the attack was 23.45hrs but some forty minutes before that nightfighters were already being concentrated around Berlin. Intercepted wireless traffic, in the form of a running commentary on the progress of the

57

The crew of No.77 Squadron Halifax JD379/KN-M, share a joke with WAAFs at Elvington prior to setting off for Hamburg.
(L-R): Sergeant Reg Croft (flight engineer); Sergeant Alan Pears (bomb aimer); Flying Officer Charlie Rollings (rear gunner); Pilot Officer Philip Stiff, with mascot (wireless operator); Sergeant Charlie Brister (mid-upper gunner); Flight Sergeant Alex Massie (pilot). Navigator Bill Plunkett was still at briefing when this picture was taken. (C. Brister)

bomber stream, indicated that German Fighter Controllers believed as early as 22.38hrs that the capital city might be the target. At 23.04hrs all fighters were ordered to proceed there. It is believed that of the estimated total of thirty-three bombers that succumbed to fighter attack, two-thirds of them went down in the target area.

Halifax *KN-M* was one of them: it was intercepted by a nightfighter and was shot down near Celle. Alex Massie, Alan Pears and Charlie Rollings died in the crash. Charlie Brister, one of the survivors, describes what happened:

'The tail gunner gave a bit of a warning; he reckoned he'd picked up fighters in the area. We kept a good lookout and the pilot started weaving – but not violently. Then, when we thought we were clear and had been flying normally again for a few minutes, we got clobbered underneath without warning. We didn't see or hear anything until the rattle of a couple of good bursts. They hit us in the port wing, somewhere between the two engines, and it was only a few seconds before it burst into flames. The fire in the tanks got gradually bigger and bigger, until it trailed back nearly to the tailplane, passing right by my turret. I shouted to Alec, "We'll have to get the hell out of here: she's on fire!" Alec put the nose down and tried to dive the fire out, but it didn't work. I took it for granted that it would be a bale out, though I never heard the order given.

' The tail gunner, Charlie Rollings, and myself had an arrangement that we would try to help each other if we ever got into difficulties. I only got one side of my parachute clipped on and was on my way down to the rear turret when the plane started to rock about: I think the controls were burning away. I opened the main door as I went down to the tail turret. I got almost to the turret when the nose of the aircraft dropped suddenly and I was thrown back to the cross beam, just aft of the mid-upper turret. The aircraft was spinning by now and I couldn't get back to the tail turret. After a struggle, I got the rest of my parachute pack clipped on. I managed to get my feet out of the door, sitting on the floor, and the slipstream actually whipped me out of the aircraft. As I went past the tail, I noticed that the whole tail section was on fire: I think the burning petrol had set the tail alight. The fin on the port side had practically gone.

Sergeant Charlie Brister
mid-upper gunner. C. Brister

'From then on it was "wait a little and then pull the cord". I was swearing like the devil at the fact that I was having to bale out over Germany; I wanted to go home. Coming down, I saw another parachute canopy below me. I collapsed the air out of one side of my parachute and tried to slide down to this other parachute. I must have come down almost to him, because when I landed in some trees, Croftie, the engineer, was only a few yards away.'

Reg Croft, Bill Plunkett and Charlie Brister were captured and spent

*The wreck of Halifax JD379/KN-M (No.77 Squadron Elvington) which was shot down near Celle on the night of 23/24 August, 1943. (*IWM HO 25822*)*

the rest of the war in Camp 4B, Muhlberg (Elbe); Philip Stiff shared a similar fate at Stalag Luft 3. Two other Halifaxes failed to return to Elvington that night: JD465/*KN-O* (Squadron Leader NW Wright) and BB238/*KN-Y* (Sergeant AR Baxter). Their fate is currently unknown.

Postscript

No.77 Squadron detailed twenty-four Halifaxes for the raid on Berlin on 23/24 August, 1943. Three failed to take off and four returned early, due to technical problems. Of the fourteen aircraft that went on to bomb the target, three failed to return − a loss rate of 21.4 per cent.

20/21 December, 1943

Frankfurt was the main target on the night of 20/21 December, 1943, when 650 bombers were detailed for the raid. Among the aircraft taking part that night was Halifax Mk V *KN-H* (No.LL127) of No.77 Squadron, Elvington. It was crewed by Warrant Officer EA Brown (pilot); Sergeant PL Jeffrey (2nd pilot); Sergeant NE Rudge (navigator); Flight Sergeant M Tarpey (bomb aimer); Flight Sergeant Dillnutt (wireless operator); Sergeant P Davison (flight engineer); Sergeant AR Wellburn (mid-upper gunner); and Sergeant RA Green (rear gunner).

German fighter controllers plotted the attacking force all the way to the target and there were many interceptions by nightfighters along the route. The Lancasters and Halifaxes that survived such combats then had to face the searchlights and the flak over the target area. 41 bombers (287 aircrew) failed to return: twenty-seven of those were Halifaxes of No.4 Group.

'Ernie' Brown and four of his crew were among the lucky ones — but their trip was not without incident.

KN-H was almost over the target when a burst of tracer from an unseen nightfighter barely missed them. Brown's response was immediate, but as he banked steeply to starboard in an evasive manoeuvre '...another stream of bullets stitched the whole of the port wing and fuselage...' wounding two of the crew, cutting off the intercom and jamming the ailerons. At its altitude of 18,000ft the Halifax rolled into a slow, spinning dive from which recovery was by no means certain.

While he wrestled to restore control, and with escape as the first priority, Brown shouted and gestured that the crew were to bale out. He remembers that when the navigator, wireless operator and the second-pilot jumped at 12,000ft the controls were still locked, but then:

'...the Flight Engineer scrambled his way to me with his thumb raised and the intercom came on. Then the controls became free so I cancelled the order to abandon and began a gentle recovery, climbing back to 12,000ft and regaining our course.

The attack (on Frankfurt) had developed so we assessed our position and found that the hydraulics opened only the wing bomb-doors and, with a 2,000lb bomb in the main bay, I was somewhat at a loss what to do. However, we bombed with all we could release and turned for home.

Once in the clear and back in darkness we made a more careful check: three crew members gone; no navigational aids; IFF unserviceable; no main radio; all Engineer's gauges shattered; and the Flight Engineer and the Mid-Upper Gunner wounded. A pretty sorry state to be in so far from home.'

With two wounded crew members on board and a 2,000lb bomb in the bomb-bay, the alternatives of bale-out or crash-land were discarded. In the event, all four engines were working smoothly and so the crew opted to try to make it home. Once over the sea, and when they considered themselves safe from prowling fighters, they circled around until, after considerable difficulty, they eventually released the bomb and set course for Coltishall, where:

> '...With no flaps, hydraulics or manual undercarriage..., we went in for a belly landing. The "Bungee cable", which no-one really believed in, gave us a perfect result.'

Brown was awarded an immediate DFC for his efforts that night; for their efforts on the return journey, Tarpey and Green were awarded immediate DFMs.

Subsequent to their promotions, Pilot Officer EA Brown DFC (centre), Warrant Officer M Tarpey DFM (left) and Flight Sergeant RA Green of No.77 Squadron, Elvington, alongside Halifax KN-F (via H Shinkfield)

ELVINGTON

Two Free French bomber squadrons were formed at Elvington in 1944: No.346 (Guyenne) Squadron on 15 May and No.347 (Tunisie) Squadron on 20 June. Both were initially equipped with Halifax Mk Vs, but within a month these were replaced by the Mk III version, a type that both squadrons retained until March 1945, when Halifax Mk VIs were allocated to them.

No.346 (Guyenne) Squadron began operations on 1 June, 1944, when eleven of its aircraft were launched against a radar station at Ferm d'Urville; the Squadron flew its last operation on 25 April, 1945, when it sent eighteen Halifaxes to bomb the gun batteries on the Frisian island of Wangerooge. During its time with No.4 Group Bomber Command No.346 flew 1,371 sorties in 121 raids at a cost of fifteen (1.1 per cent) aircraft lost.

No.347 (Tunisie) Squadron began active service a week after being formed: on the night of 27/28 June, 1944 eleven Halifaxes were despatched against the V-weapon site at Mount Candon. Like its sister unit, No.347 ended its war operations with an attack on the island of Wangerooge on 25 April, 1945. Twelve aircraft were despatched: one failed to return. At the end of hostilities, the squadron had flown 1,355 sorties in 110 raids and, like No.346, had lost fifteen (1.1 per cent) aircraft.

The combined losses of thirty aircraft represents some 200 aircrew. The French memorial to such sacrifice is located at the south end of Elvington village and was erected in the late 1950s.

The Free French memorial, Elvington village

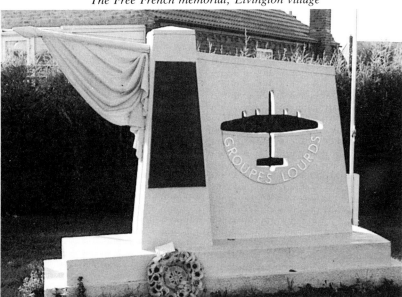

Inscription:

HERE WAS STATIONED
1944-1945
GROUPEMENT
DE
BOMBARDEMENT
No 1
COMPRISING THE
FRENCH SQUADRONS
GUYENNE AND
TUNISIE
R.A.F SQUADRONS
346-347

ICI STATIONNA EN
1944-1945
LE GROUPEMENT DE
BOMBARDEMENT
No 1
COMPRENANT LES
GROUPS FRANCAIS
GUYENNE ET
TUNISIE
SQUADRONS DE LA R.A.F
346-347

This monument recalls
their battle and the
sacrifice of their dead

Ce monument rapelle
leurs combats et le
sacrifice de leurs morts

17/18 December, 1944

Bomber Command detailed 523 aircraft to attack Duisberg on the night of 17/18 December, 1944. Among those taking part was a Halifax Mk III of No.346 (Guyenne) Squadron, Elvington, piloted by Sous Lieutenant Georges Rames.

Bad weather on 17 December had twice delayed the briefing for the operation and it was not until conditions improved in the early hours of the following day that the raid got underway, Rames' aircraft lifting off from Elvington at 3.00 am. The weather offered no problems until the Halifax had crossed the French coast: shortly after that, the bomber entered the dense cloud which was to persist all the way to the target.

The average outside temperature of -38 degrees caused severe − but generally manageable − icing which affected control surfaces and rendered the windscreen opaque. For the two-and-a-half-hour trip from the Channel to the target, Rames was dependent on his blind-flying instruments. However, so long as those instruments functioned the Halifax was able to retain the protection that the cloud offered against marauding nightfighters.

The cloud persisted over Duisburg and so navigator Captain Henri Petit operated the Gee Box and instructed bomb-aimer Andre Dezellis when they were over the target. They released their bomb-load of 9,500lbs at 6.31am from an altitude of 18,500ft and with their mission accomplished, the Frenchmen altered course for home − and for trouble.

Some four minutes after leaving the target area, Rames was in the process of following his navigator's instructions and banking on to a new heading when he noticed that the artificial horizon instrument was acting strangely. When he attempted to ease the Halifax out of the banking maneouvre there was no response from the controls. Seemingly, ice had jammed the ailerons and the bomber, instead of levelling out, went into a left-hand spin and a dive that soon exceeded 400mph.

The flight engineer, Adjutant Rene Bauer, was quick to realize that the cause of the instrument failure was the seizure of the vacuum pump that served it, but he could not reach the emergency pump switch because he was pinned to his seat by centrifugal force. In spite of any effort Rames could make, the altimeter began to unwind with increasing speed.

Fearing that a crash was inevitable, rear gunner Jean Le Guillou took to his parachute; for the same reason Henri Petit helped his bomb-aimer to bale out from the forward escape hatch. With Denzellis safely away, and with 30-tons of Halifax still spiralling earthwards, Petit laboriously clawed his way up to the cockpit, clutching at any hand-hold on the fuselage wall to avoid being dashed to the floor by the centrifugal force.

As he forced his way upwards, he inadvertently grabbed the ripcord of Rames's parachute, which was hanging against the fuselage wall to the pilot's right. The pack spilled open and the onrush of air from the jettisoned hatch deployed the canopy along the entire length of the inside fuselage: for the pilot, at least, bale out had ceased to be an option.

Perhaps the disappearance of his alternative escape route focussed Rames's attention even more. Rising from his seat and bracing his back against the armour plating, the pilot stamped both feet on the right rudder pedal and exerted all of the strength at his disposal in an effort to arrest the spiral, regain control and ease his aircraft into level flight. It took an age − and when he eventually succeeded he had only seconds to spare. The altimeter registered 1,000ft when Rames was able to ease back the stick: the speed generated by the descent allowed the Halifax to recover to 2,700ft.

When they were once more in stable flight, Bauer was able to connect the emergency vacuum pump, but thirty minutes were to elapse before the blind-flying instruments began to react. Before that happened the flyers would have other problems to contend with.

The first came minutes after the pilot had regained control after the Halifax had plummeted 17,000ft: they were caught by a burst of 40mm flak, which peppered the front of the aircraft. Wireless operator Robert Mimaud had his right arm almost severed below the elbow and suffered additional wounds to his legs and buttocks; Raoul Vidal, the mid-upper gunner, received a six-inch scalp wound. One shell struck a fuse box and rendered useless the D/R compass, the Gee Box, the radio, the intercom, lighting and IFF, while the magnetic compass '...was spinning like a top...'

While Petit and Bauer tended to the wounded, Rames considered his position: two crew members (including the rear gunner) had baled out and Vidal (the mid-upper gunner) was too badly wounded to be effective, thus the Halifax was defenceless; the wireless operator was severely wounded; Petit, the navigator had a badly sprained ankle and − more seriously − had been traumatized by the events of the preceding minutes and was not functioning properly as a navigator; because of the inability to fly blind (at least until the necessary instruments began to respond they would have to fly just below the cloud base altitude of 1,000ft − a risky business at any time over wartime Europe; and they were without intercom, radio and compass, which meant that they could not communicate internally or externally − and they did not really know the *direction* in which they were heading.

They had been flying on their existing track for some twenty minutes when Bauer suggested the use of the 30mm diameter compass in the crew escape box as an aid to navigation. Incredibly, with the help of that small device they were able to calculate that they were roughly sout-east of Soest. Thus ever since their encounter with the flak they had been flying *eastwards* and deeper into Germany. As Georges Rames was later to recall, they '...had flown almost the full length of the Ruhr − then considered to be the most strongly defended area in the world − at no more than 1,000ft and had got away with it...'

On the strength of readings from the pocket compass, they altered

Halifax B Mk VII (NP763/H7-N) of 346 (Guyenne) Squadron, Free French Air Force, Elvington. (Imperial War Museum HU1978)

course to 270 degrees and flew westwards. Though a number of searchlights endeavoured to seek them out, luck was with them and they re-crossed the Ruhr's northern sector without incident. Over Holland, the cloud base was down to six hundred feet and searchlights in the occupied zones almost fingered them on two occasions – but their luck held, aided, perhaps, by the Halifax's low altitude.

Dawn was breaking as they approached the Dutch coast and they were able to establish visually that they were south of the Zuider Zee. Rames set course for Manston, via Walcheren Island and Ostend. By then, they were flying over areas occupied by the Allies and thus the dangers were less serious although by no means over, for trigger-happy gunners lacking aircraft recognition skills had been known to shoot first and to ask questions later. It was precisely for that reason that when he was over the Channel George Rames temporarily deviated from his course in order to avoid over-flying a convoy. Shortly afterwards, they landed at Manston, touch-down being preceded by a red flare fired by Bauer to warn of their difficulties.

When it was all over and the wounded had been cared for, Rames and Bauer inspected their aircraft. They discovered that flak had punched some two hundred holes in the front right side of the bomber and that the cockpit had been holed by several shards of shrapnel and three 40mm shells. With Rames sitting in his pilot's seat – and with the aid of a stick inserted through the points of entry and exit of the flak – they were able to calculate that one of the shells must have passed within centimetres of the pilot's face.

If luck had not been with George Rames that night, it is unlikely that this tale would have been written. However, not all of his crew survived the ordeal. Of the two members who baled out, Andre Dezellis landed safely but spent the rest of the war as a POW; rear-gunner Jean Le Gillou had less good fortune – he was never seen again.

3/4 March, 1945

Although the Elvington-based French squadrons commenced operations at a time when the Allies were establishing air superiority and bomber loss rates were falling, catastrophe was never far away. Usually, the threat came in the skies over Europe, from fighters of the *Luftwaffe* and from flak – the combined efforts of which accounted for five (31 per cent) bombers of No.346 (Guyenne) Squadron on the night of 4/5 November, 1944 (see page 18). However, sometimes the threat was nearer home.

Bombers were most vulnerable to attack when they were returning from operations and preparing to land. Then, the concentration that had kept men safe was beginning to wane and the mind was starting to address other things; crews were tired, more relaxed and less on guard. Additionally, decreasing altitude as aircraft made their approaches to base meant that there was less room for manoeuvre in the event of interception by nightfighters.

Throughout the war, both the RAF and the *Luftwaffe* had ambushed crews returning from operations, but the Germans had never exploited the strategy on quite the same scale as their opponents. However, on the night of 3/4 March, 1945, German nightfighters launched *Operation Gisela* against Lancasters and Halifaxes which were returning from a raid on the synthetic oil plants at Kamen.

At around midnight, some one hundred Ju88s crossed the English coast line on a wide front that stretched from Essex to Yorkshire and infiltrated the bomber streams. The attacks that followed took their toll and when the last nightfighter left some two hours later twenty-four bombers had been shot down and a further twenty had been damaged. Three of the Halifaxes shot down by intruders belonged to the French.

The crew of Halifax NA680/*H7-H* (No.347 Squadron) were returning from their first operation when they were caught over the Wash. They were attacked on three separate occasions and managed to evade twice, but on the third encounter their starboard inner engine was set on fire. The pilot, Captain Lacou, and flight engineer, Sergeant LeMasson, controlled the Halifax long enough for the rest of the crew to bale out but left themselves with no time to follow suit. Both were killed when their aircraft crashed in flames at Sleaford, Lincolnshire, at 1.05am on 4 March.

Ten minutes later, No.347 Squadron Halifax NR235/*H7-Q* crashed in flames at Sutton-on-Derwent. Squadron Leader J Terrien and his crew had already witnessed a No.466 Squadron Halifax fall to earth near Elvington and had escaped one attack on their aircraft when they were intercepted a second time. When the starboard wing started to blaze there was no option but to bale out. Six of the crew took to their parachutes but Terrien was still at the controls when the Halifax went down. It was his twenty-eighth operation.

The crew of No.346 Squadron Halifax NR229/*L8-D* had rather better luck when they were diverted northwards to Croft, which was considered to be safer than Elvington. However, they were intercepted as pilot Captain Notelle was at 900ft altitude and making his approach to the airfield. The nightfighter's attack caused fire to break out in one wing of the bomber, but lack of altitude left no room for a bale out with safety. Notelle opted for a forced landing, from which all escaped. However, the unconscious Captain had to be carried away by his crew as flames enveloped the wreck.

HOLME-ON-SPALDING MOOR

The project for the memorial that now stands at the entrance to the old airfield at Holme-on-Spalding-Moor was conceived in 1986, when a reunion of ex-Squadron members was held at Holme. One of the leading proponents of the scheme was the first chairman of the No.76 Squadron Association, Bill Day.

The monument was financed by Association members and was unveiled on Sunday 20 September, 1987, during the dedication ceremony conducted by Canon Jack Armstrong. The unveiling was carried out by Group Captain Leonard Cheshire, VC DSO DFC, a former commander of the squadron, who also took the salute at a march-past of ex-No.76 Squadron personnel.

The following inscription appears below the squadron crest and above a list of the Squadron's Second World War battle honours.

No.76 Squadron memorial, Holme-on-Spalding Moor

IN REMEMBRANCE

of those aircrew members from the United Kingdom, Australia, New Zealand, Canada and Norway, who gave their lives in the cause of freedom in operational sorties against the enemy from

76 Squadron 1941-1945

and to the ground personnel who lost their lives by enemy action

They gave their today for our tomorrow We who survived give thanks to Almighty God We will remember them

On 4 July, 1993, the Squadron Association added to their memorials when they unveiled a plaque in the entrance to the St. George's Hotel, Tees-side Airport, to commemorate the Squadron's time spent at the

August, 1941. Halifax BI (L9530/MP-L) being serviced at Middleton-St-George. This aircraft failed to return from Berlin on the night of 13 August, 1941.

airfield from June 1941 to September 1943, when the airport was RAF Middleton-St-George.

No.76 Squadron had fought during the First World War but had been disbanded in 1919. It was reformed at Finningley in April 1937 and was equipped with Wellesley bombers. It subsequently underwent two disbandments prior to 1 May, 1941, when it was reformed at Linton for a period of continuous service which would last until 1 September, 1946.

Following its re-formation at Linton, No. 76 Squadron was initially equipped with Halifax Is. It became operational in June 1941, when it moved to Middleton-St-George and equipped with Halifax Mk IIs. In September 1942 the Squadron returned to Linton and in February 1943 changed to Halifax Vs. The final wartime move occurred on 16 June, 1943, with the posting to Holme-on-Spalding Moor. No.76 changed aircraft types twice whilst at Holme: in January 1944 (Halifax Mk III) and March 1945 (Halifax Mk VI).

During its war service, No.76 Squadron carried out 396 bombing raids (5,123 sorties), − the highest number recorded by any Halifax unit − at a cost of 139 aircraft (2.7 per cent), including sixteen in crashes in Britain. Total crew losses amounted to 787 killed and 278 made prisoners of war. The scale of the carnage might be gauged from the fact that in 1943 the Squadron lost fifty-nine aircraft (three times its operational strength) in 104 nights of operations, an average of one aircraft every two nights. This loss rate was surpassed in January 1944 when the Squadron lost eight aircraft (almost half its operational strength) in two nights.

5/6 September, 1943

On the night of 5/6 September, 1943, 605 aircraft were despatched to Mannheim/Ludwigshafen, in south-west Germany. The attackers lost thirty-four aircraft (5.6 per cent). No.76 Squadron, Holme-on-Spalding Moor, contributed 22 aircraft, one of which was destined not to return.

Halifax MK V DK223/*MP-N* was lost to a nightfighter and crashed north-east of Saarbrücken, between the villages of Waldmohr and Jägersburg. The bomber was already in some difficulty before the interception occurred, pilot Pilot Officer Schmidt having had to close down the inner starboard engine and feather the propeller because of fire. When the fighter attacked, the port inner engine was hit and the port fuel tanks set ablaze. The crew were preparing to evacuate the aircraft when the nightfighter made its second approach. It was then that Pilot Officer Schmidt was heard to gasp, '...as though hit, and the aircraft plunged into a dive...'

Navigator Flying Officer Goldberg and bomb-aimer Pilot Officer AF Smith managed to bale out through the nose hatch seconds before the bomber exploded — with such force that the fuselage was split in two along its entire length. Flying Officer Goldberg, having narrowly escaped one danger, fell victim to the blast: when his body was found close by the wreck, it was still attached to his fully deployed parachute. Sergeants EV Dean, AF Walling, WH Saunders and AF Todd were the other crew members who died.

The wreck of the Halifax Mk V DK223/MP-N *(No.76 Squadron, Holme-on-Spalding Moor) which fell victim to a nightfighter and crashed near Saarbrücken on the night of 5/6 September, 1943.* (Uwe Benkel)

Pilot Officer Smith survived to become a prisoner of war; his friends were buried in Choloy cemetery, where they still lie.

'Day after day during the war we watched our Halifaxes with their gallant crews taking off for their hazardous missions. Very few of them survived. In the worst times of 1943 and 1944 as few as 20 per cent or less could expect to complete a tour of thirty operations. During the nights of 20th and 21st January 1944 we lost eight aircraft and thirty-nine aircrew. Our memorials, therefore, are a small token and tribute in remembrance of colleagues and friends who did not live "To See the Dawn Breaking".

'Paddy' Reed, WAAF Sergeant, Operations Room, Holme-on-Spalding Moor, 1942-45

(Uwe Benkel)

LISSETT

The possibility of erecting a memorial to all personnel – both ground-crew and air-crew – who had served at Lissett was first discussed by members of the No.158 Squadron Association during 1982/83 when, it was felt, evidence of Lissett's wartime activities was fast disappearing as the site was increasingly converted to industrial and agricultural uses. Thus a Memorial Committee was established and it achieved its purpose one year later.

The memorial to No.158 Squadron stands at the entrance to the churchyard of St. James of Compostela, Lissett. It takes the form of a rough hewn block of sandstone inset with a plaque of crown metal. The outline of a Halifax bomber in relief is centrally placed below the inscription.

It was unveiled on 9 September, 1984, by Wing Commander Peter Dobson, DSO DFC AFC (who had commanded the Squadron from June 1944 until March 1945) during a service officiated by the Bishop of Hull, the Right Reverend Donald Snelgrove. The salute of the march past that followed was taken by Group Captain Tom Sawyer DFC, one of Lissett's Station Commanders during the Second World War.

No.158 Squadron was re-formed for wartime service at Driffield on 14 February, 1942 and was equipped with Wellington Mk II bombers until June of that year, when the Squadron changed over to the Halifax Mk II following a move to East Moor. Lissett aerodrome, near Bridlington, was officially opened as part of No.4 Group, Bomber Command, in late February 1943. No.158 Squadron moved there on 28 February, 1943, having spent the preceding four months at Rufforth. The Squadron flew the Halifax Mk III from December 1943 until April 1945, when the Mk VI version was adopted.

During the Second World War, No.158 Squadron carried out 5,371 sorties in 382 raids, from which 156 (2.9 per cent) aircraft failed to return; in addition, a further thirty-nine aircraft were destroyed as a result of crashes in this country. 334 awards for gallantry were awarded as a consequence of such operations, but 851 personnel lost their lives while in Squadron service.

31 August, 1943

On the night of 31 August, 1943, 622 bombers were launched against Berlin. Forty-seven aircraft failed to return from the operation, a loss rate of 7.6 percent. No.158 Squadron, Lissett, contributed nineteen Halifaxes and lost four (21 percent) of them.

One of the four was a Halifax Mk II (HR776/*NP-R*) crewed by Sergeant K Ward (pilot); Sergeant N Stubbings (navigator); Sergeant AP Arnott (bomb aimer); Sergeant RA Thurston (wireless operator); Sergeant T Craven (mid-upper gunner) Sergeant H Simister (flight engineer); and Sergeant N Avery (rear gunner). They were on their twenty-first bombing operation when they were caught directly over the target by a nightfighter, just after the bombs had been released and the bomb-doors had closed.

Nightfighters were out in force over the target area and their deadly pupose was aided by numerous illuminating flares that turned night into day. One such chandelier of brilliant incandescence mushroomed directly behind Ward's Halifax, its blinding glare masking the approach of an attacking Focke-Wulf 190. Rear gunner 'Nicky' Avery managed to scream 'Corkscrew!' to his pilot and to return the attacker's fire a micro-second before Ward's violent evasive actions wrenched the bomber free and the fighter vanished into the night. Then the rear gunner saw tongues of flame streaming down the port side of his turret.

Avery's warning alerted the crew almost at the same time as the fighter's cannon shells found the bomber's port engines‘ and set them on fire. Harry Simister feathered the propellers and tried to extinguish the blaze – but long before the flames were doused probing searchlights fastened on to the Halifax, emphasizing its presence. The second attack came from below, just as Ward was ordering his crew to prepare to bale out: again cannon shells pumped

Harry Simister, flight engineer, No.158 Squadron, Lissett, (H. Simister)

into the aircraft, setting the fuselage ablaze and causing the bomber to slip away from the pilot's control and begin its plunge earthwards; above the sound of the two remaining engines, Harry Simister heard the sound of bullets ripping through metal and felt numbing pains in his chest and in his leg. Ken Ward had just enough time to yell 'Bale out!' before the intercom went dead and the emergency evacuation light began flashing.

As the bomber's dive steepened, Harry Simister felt a tugging at his clothing and in the flickering light he saw Ron Thurston beckoning him down to the escape hatch in the nose. By the time the flight engineer had strapped on his parachute and had made his way to the exit, three of his crewmates had already gone. 'Stubby' Stubbings was the first to go, quickly followed by Percy Arnott: Ron Thurston went next – but only after he had grabbed his parachute as it rolled towards the escape hatch and hastily fastened it to his harness. Ken Ward was still wrestling with the controls as Harry Simister moved towards the exit. As he passed, he gave his pilot the parachute that was normally stored on the nearby bulkhead – and then he put his trust in a piece of silk and launched himself into the night.

Because of fire in the fuselage, Nicky Avery had no option but to exit via his turret, which he rotated ninety degrees to port before throwing himself backwards into the void. However, instead of falling away, he found himself being dragged along at the back of the aircraft. One of his feet was trapped and it was only after desperate moments that he managed to wriggle it free from his flying boot and separate himself from the machine.

Three of the crew lost their lives that night. The pilot and the mid-upper gunner died shortly after Harry Simister baled out: the Halifax blew up '...taking poor old Ken and Tommy with it'; Percy Arnott was killed when he fell to earth after his parachute failed to open.

The rest were destined to survive, though 'Stubby' Stubbings had his own dicey moment. A non-swimmer, he landed in a large lake just outside of Berlin and found himself in real danger of drowning in the time it took to finally discard his parachute harness and inflate his *Mae West*. Half-drowned, he splashed about for hours before finally reaching land, where he was arrested by farmworkers. Rear gunner Nicky Avery landed heavily in a street, hurting his foot in the process. In a state of some shock he knocked on a door, asked for assistance – and was handed over to the police. Ron Thurston landed heavily in open county and sprained an ankle: he was apprehended in the Potsdam area the next day (his bale out is described more fully in the following pages). Harry Simister landed safely enough some twelve miles from the target and was relieved to find that his wounds were only minor. Showing great initiative, he stole a bicycle and began what amounted to an impromptu tour of the port areas of Northern Germany in the hope of finding a

Ron Thurston, wireless operator, No.158 Squadron, Lissett. (R. Thurston)

neutral ship that might offer refuge and the chance of escape. His efforts were unsuccessful and so he decided to cycle to Spain! However, while passing through the Low Countries he established contact with the Dutch Resistance and eventually arrived back in England a little over twelve months after his bale out over Berlin. He was later awarded the Military Medal for his endeavours.

Baling out over Berlin

Ron Thurston, 158 Squadron, Lissett, baled out of his crippled Halifax (HR776/*NP-R*) over Berlin on the night of 31 August, 1943, after being attacked by a nightfighter. His thoughts as he parachuted to safety were graphically described in his article *Baling out over Berlin*, which was published in the Aircrew Association's *Intercom* (Autumn 1988):

'Baling out of a blazing bomber over Berlin, one of the most heavily defended cities in Germany, could possibly be described as baling out of hell into hell, as I experienced at midnight on 31 August, 1943 when ...(my) Halifax bomber...was attacked directly over the target by enemy nightfighters seconds after the bombs were dropped and immediately the bomb doors closed. Seconds earlier and the whole crew would have perished instead of only three...

To bale out of a blazing bomber still under attack, with two engines on fire, completely out of control, coned by searchlights, among 600 bombers dropping bombs from various heights, (and among) nightfighters, flares, and bursting shells, gave thoughts to the extreme danger when the parachute opened and gently drifted away from the nightmare of the target. Thoughts, in the dark and dangerous sky, of the fate of the rest of the crew. How many had been killed in this hell? You look around in the sky for parachutes. You see nothing. Searchlights sweep the sky, as if looking for you...

You watch with fascination the blazing target, the explosions of the bombs, and the retaliation of the anti-aircraft guns, with little thought for the thousands of tons of flak in the air.

You wonder if the tracer bullets you see are coming from an air gunner's turret, or from an enemy fighter attacking another bomber. You watch with dismay a blazing bomber plunging down to earth and you wonder if anyone got out.

Your parachute seems to be going up instead of coming down, and you feel slightly sick with the swaying. You begin to wonder what height you are at when you see a nightfighter only a little way above you...and (you wonder) where you will hit the ground. Will you be shot when you are in the hands of the enemy? Or shown mercy as a POW? All these thoughts as you slowly, alone, and completely helpless, descend into the unknown. Your face feels wet with perspiration – or is it raining? You feel a little numb in this dark, unreal world and wonder if you are dreaming. The crunch of an anti-aircraft shell nearby tells you that you are not...

You listen to the humming engines of the bombers. Some will be shot down on the way home, perhaps over the sea.

All the way back to the English coast – and sometimes inland – they will be pursued by determined enemy nightfighters, with their excellent radar and equally brave pilots... The bomber crews are alert to this and do not relax for one moment.

You are mesmerized by the red glow in the sky from the fires, observing the flashes from the anti-aircraft guns and the shell bursts…you begin to think of your loved ones back home. In a few hours they will receive that dreaded telegram that they have been expecting ever since you started operational flying – *Regret to inform that your…* and you begin to wonder whether you will ever see them again…'

24/25 March, 1944

Sergeant Harry Ball trained as a wireless operator/air gunner and in December 1943, at the age of 21, he was posted to his first operational unit, No.158 Squadron, Lissett, which was equipped with the Halifax Mk III.

Prior to 24 March, 1944, he went on eleven operational sorties, the first of which his crew aborted after fifty minutes when two engines packed up; the second of which cost the lives of two crew members following a low-level bale out when two engines again seized up during a return from Magdeburg; two of which resulted in over-shooting the runway following brake failure; and one occasion when they returned to base with a 1,000 pound bomb hung up in the bomb bay.

Those eleven operations cost Bomber Command 243 aircraft (and some 1,600 aircrew). Generally speaking, Ball's crew had been lucky – but on 24/25 March, 1944, when 811 bombers were launched against Berlin, their luck ran out. Bomber Command lost 72 aircraft on that operation, and Harry Ball's Halifax (LW721/*NP-S*) was one of them.

The trip to the target was uneventful but at 21,000ft over the 'Big City', and just after their bombs had been released, they were attacked from below by a Junkers 88 nightfighter equipped with the upward-firing cannons, known as *Schräge Musik.*

Cannon shells ripped into the Halifax, wounding Flight Sergeant McDonagh, the bomb aimer, and setting two engines on fire. Seconds later, McDonagh was struck again when the nightfighter followed up his first attack and cannon shells caused fire to break out in the fuselage. As the bomber dipped earthwards, out of control and threatening to go into a spin, pilot Flight Sergeant Van Slyke yelled a warning over the intercom: 'For Christ's sake, get out of this aircraft!'

Harry Ball, Wireless operator/AG, No.158 Squadron, Lissett. (H. Ball)

Realising that the Halifax could explode at any moment, Harry reached for the parachute he had stored in its usual place on the wall close to his compartment and struggled to secure it to his harness – a task achieved only with difficulty because of the bomber's wild gyrations. Then he made his way towards the forwards escape hatch.

By that time, Sergeant Grant, the mid-upper gunner, and Pilot Officer A McGillivary, the navigator, had baled out. Had there been time for such thoughts, Harry might have expected the rear gunner, Flight Sergeant Mardon-Mowbray, to have followed suit by turning his turret through ninety degrees and exiting backwards. However, such a rotation of the rear turret required hydraulic power or, if that were not available, the use of a manually-operated lever. Either would have done – but it seems likely that the nightfighter's cannon shells had damaged Mardon-Mowbray's station: he was trapped and in desperate trouble. As Harry was moving towards the nose he heard the rear gunner screaming, 'I can't get out of my turret!' But with the plane going into a spin there was no way in which the wireless operator could have got to the rear of the aircraft to help.

Ball made his exit via the front escape hatch. When his parachute opened and he had time to take stock he knew that his problems were far from over: he was suspended above the burning city of Berlin and there was a possibility of landing there:

'I could see that all the earth below me was on fire. I knew that if I landed in that then if the fires didn't finish me off the civilians would...' but '...there were strong winds that night and I drifted away into the blackness...I made a nice soft landing in the middle of a dyke. The March winds were strong...and I was pulled along by my 'chute for quite a distance before I could release myself. With the soaking I got I must have looked like a drowned rat. In the end, that is how I was when the Germans caught me.'

Grant, McGillivary and McDonagh, were also captured and, like Harry, spent the remaining period of hostilites as prisoners of war – but the other members of the crew were not so fortunate. Some time was to

29 June, 1943. Lissett aerodrome from 11,000ft. (via David E. Thompson)

pass before Ball learned of their fate, and then he found himself speculating about the last moments of Halifax *NP-S*:

'Later on I heard that three bodies had been found in a burnt out Halifax: Van Slyke (pilot), Whitelaw (engineer) and Mardon-Mowbray (rear gunner) had gone down with the plane. Was it possible that the pilot was badly wounded, or that he had stayed at the controls to give the rear gunner a better chance of getting out of his turret, and left it too late?'

Whether or not Van Slyke and the others had hesitated too long – or, perhaps, had found themselves captive to the centrigual force of the spinning bomber – will never be known: *their* story, like so many others of men who served with Bomber Command, cannot be told...

Pilot Officer KS Simpson and his crew of Halifax III LW718/*NP-T* set out for Berlin at 6.55pm, five minutes after Van Slyke's crew. At 10.40pm Simpson radioed to base that he was over the Dutch coast, that one port engine and one starboard engine had suffered malfunctions and that he was returning to base.

It is not known what dangers Simpson and his crew overcame during their trip across the North Sea, but they managed to make landfall near Cromer, where the pilot set down his aircraft close to the water's edge. Simpson could not possibly have known that the site chosen for his crash-landing had been sown with mines years before. The Halifax landed in the minefield at 11.11pm and blew up, killing all members of the crew: Pilot Officer KS Simpson (pilot); Flying Officer N Hindley (navigator); Pilot Officer DJ Hemsley (bomb aimer); Sergeant Barnett (flight engineer); Flight Sergeant Suddaby (wireless operator); Sergeant WA Buchan (mid-upper gunner); Flight Sergeant MF McKay (rear gunner).

Harry Ball's crew on arrival at No.158 Squadron, Lissett, December 1943. L-R: Sergeant JN McDonagh (bomb aimer); Sergeant L Collingwood (rear gunner); Sergeant R Whitelaw (flight engineer); Flight Sergeant AR Van Slyke (pilot); Sergeant H Ball (wireless operator); Pilot Officer A McGillivary (navigator); Sergeant Grant (mid-upper gunner).
Sergeant Collingwood was killed on the return trip from Magdeburg, 21/22 January, 1944; Sergeant Whitelaw and Flight Sergeant Van Slyke lost their lives over Berlin on 24/25 March, 1944 when their aircraft was shot down; Flight Sergeant McDonagh was badly wounded by cannon-fire on the same trip and, together with Sergeant Ball, Pilot Officer McGillivary and Sergeant Grant, spent the rest of the war as a POW. Two additional members, not shown here, lost their lives while serving with Van Slyke's crew: a 'spare' navigator called Evans, who died on the Magdeburg trip; and Flight Sergeant K Mardon-Mowbray (rear gunner), who was trapped in his turret over Berlin on 24/25 March, 1944, and crashed with his aircraft.
(H.Ball)

ATWICK nr HORNSEA

12-year-old Georgina Wood, was the special guest of honour when Bomber Command veterans of No.158 Squadron, Lissett, met in Bridlington in September 1994 for their annual reunion. It was their way of expressing their gratitude for the young girl's dedication to the memory of seven years of the Squadron who lost their lives thirty-eight years before she was born.

A year earlier, Georgina had been walking her dogs in a field near her home at Atwick, near Hornsea, when she discovered a neglected memorial plaque set in the middle of a bridleway. On it was carved the names of seven airmen who had perished at the site when their aircraft had crashed there on 20 February, 1944.

The aircraft was Halifax Mk III HX351/*NP-S*, one of fifteen bombers of No.158 Squadron, Lissett, which set out for Leipzig on the night of 19/20 February, 1944. Its crew was: Pilot Officer Peter Milton Jennings (pilot); Pilot Officer Norman Caffery (navigator); Flight Sergeant Gerald Robert Fitzsimmons (rear-gunner); Sergeant George Frank Gillings (wireless operator); Flight Sergeant Harold Elfed Jones (bomb aimer); Sergeant Samuel Pryce Morris (mid-upper gunner); and Pilot Officer Charles Joseph Seymour (flight engineer).

A total of 823 aircraft were detailed for the raid – and they had their share of bad luck. The bomber force was intercepted by nightfighters as it crossed the Dutch coast and was under constant harrassment all the way to the target. Seventy-eight (9.5%) aircraft – and 546 aircrew – failed to return. It is believed that some fifty aircraft were shot down by fighters, while a further four were lost in collisions and twenty succumbed to flak.

However, Jennings' aircraft was not one of those lost over Europe that night: *NP-S* did not even clear the English coastline three miles east of Lissett.

It is believed that shortly after take-off the aircraft developed an electrical fault in its elevators. Minutes later the fully-laden Halifax stalled and then nose-dived into what was then known as Dixon's field at Little Atwick, three miles north of Catfoss. It exploded on impact and burst into flames, the intensity of which made rescue attempts impossible.

The tall unit, containing Canadian rear-gunner Gerald Fitzsimmons, broke away from the main fuselage when the Halifax struck and was

Norman Caffery

Harold Jones

In Loving Memory
PETER MILTON JENNINGS
NORMAN CAFFERY
GERALD ROBERT
FITZSIMMONS
ALBERTA CANADA
GEORGE FRANK GILLINGS
HAROLD ELFED JONES
SAMUEL PRYCE MORRIS
CHARLES JOSEPH SEYMOUR
158 SQD R.A.F
WHO
PERISHED HERE
20TH FEBRUARY 1944

Georgina Wood and the Atwick Plaque. (Yorkshire Post)

Frank Gillings

Peter Seymour

Gerald Fitzsimmons

not consumed by the fire that followed. However, when would-be rescuers reached it the 22-year-old occupant was dead. Gerald Fitzsimmons was later buried in Stonefall cemetery, Harrogate, where he still lies with 664 of his fellow countrymen. It is believed that the other crew members were buried in their home towns.

The black marble plaque which commemorates the tragedy was placed on the site of crash in December 1992 and was put there on behalf of Laurence Caffery, whose twenty-one year old brother Norman had been the navigator of the Halifax: the flight to Leipzig would have been his twenty-eighth operational trip.

Georgina recalls that when she and her mother discovered it:

'I saw these names and I thought they were all buried underneath the plaque. Then my mother explained that they had died in the field and I thought that it was a pity no one remembered them so I started taking flowers up there every couple of days when I was walking my dogs.'

She has been taking flowers to the memorial ever since.

Enquiries regarding the origins of the stone and the incident it commemorates were undertaken on Georgina's behalf by her great-grandfather (who served with the RAF during the war) and eventually brought her to the notice of the No.158 Squadron Association. When the veterans learned of the interest shown by the young Atwick schoolgirl they were so impressed that they decided to repay her kindness by inviting her to attend their 1994 reunion.

On Saturday 3 September she and her parents attended a special service conducted by Reverend Don May, ex-No.158 Squadron navigator, to dedicate the plaque, and the next day she laid the Association wreath at the Squadron memorial at Lissett. During the reunion luncheon which followed it was announced she had been made a Junior Associate Member of the No.158 Squadron Association.

Needless to say, Georgina's parents are very proud of their daughter.

Postscript:

It has since become known that Georgina is not the only person to lay flowers on the memorial stone: eighty year old Ray Coates, a local resident who witnessed the incident, places seven poppies there each Armistice Day.

MELBOURNE

When war was declared on 3 September, 1939, No.10 Squadron was based at Dishforth and was equipped with Whitley Mk.IV twin-engined bombers. These were exchanged for Whitley Mk.Vs in May 1940, two months before a move to Leeming, which was destined to be 'home' for some two years. The Squadron swapped its Whitleys for Halifax Mk Is and Mk IIs in December 1941 and operated both types until the following August, when it moved to Melbourne. The Halifax Mk.I was dropped at that time but the Mk.II continued to be used until March 1944, when it was replaced by the Mk III – the type which the Squadron would use until war's end.

It was from Dishforth that the Squadron launched its first operation of the war when, on the night of 8/9 September, 1939, eight of its Whitleys sallied forth to drop propaganda leaflets ('Nickels') over north-west Germany; three weeks later it participated in the first wartime flights by the RAF over Berlin when it dropped leaflets over the German capital on the night of 1/2 October, 1939. However, although No.10 was on active service almost from the beginning of hostilities, it was not until the night of 19/20 March, 1940, that it launched its first bombing raid: a force of eight Whitleys against the seaplane base at Hornum, on the island of Sylt. The aircraft taking part in that attack returned safely – but that would not always be the case.

No.10 Squadron participated in all of the major air campaigns over Europe during the Second World War. These included the Battles of the Ruhr, of Hamburg and of Berlin. The savagery of those operations may be gauged from the fact that the Battle of Berlin cost Bomber Command 212 aircraft during November-December 1943 alone. The Squadron also took part in the Battle of Normandy and in the raids against V-1 sites. Its last operation of the war took place on 25 April, 1945, when it contributed twenty Halifaxes for a daylight raid against gun batteries on the Frisian island of Wangerooge.

In the performance of their duties No.10 Squadron personnel were awarded nine DSOs, 333 DFCs and 173 DFMs. These were earned during the course of 609 raids (including sixty-one mine-laying and fifteen leaflet-dropping operations) which involved 6,233 sorties and which resulted in the loss of 156 aircraft; an average loss-rate of 2.6 percent per raid.

The losses of aircraft represent some 990 aircrew, although it is not currently known how many of this number became *casualties*. Sadly, however – given that there was a time when the operational life-expectancy of a Melbourne Halifax was a mere three months – it is highly likely that *casualties* constituted the majority.

The memorial that stands at the entrance to the old aerodrome bears witness to their sacrifice. It was financed by ex-members and friends of the Squadron, following a suggestion by Doug Dent, Chairman of No.10 Squadron Association, after he had visited the Skipton-on-Swale monument in 1984.

Designed by Norman Appleton (Guild of Aviation Artists) and erected on a piece of land donated by farmer John Rowbottom, who now owns the Melbourne site, the monument is built of bricks from buildings which once stood on the old aerodrome.

Some 500 people were present at the unveiling on 15 September 1985. It was performed by Wing Commander Len Marshall, then CO of No.10 Squadron, Brize Norton, as one of his VC 10s flew overhead in salute. The dedication of the stone by the Rural Dean of York, Cannon Jack Armstrong, Chaplain of York ATC, was followed by a march past of 100 former servicemen and women, the salute being taken by Air Chief Marshall Sir Augustus Walker, wartime base commander of the nearby Pocklington airfield.

Inscription:

No.10 SQUADRON
4 GROUP BOMBER COMMAND
W.W.II 1939-1945

This Memorial was erected at the entrance to the former RAF Station Melbourne by the ex Members and Friends of the Squadron to honour the memory of all personnel who died in the service of their Country during WW II and as a tribute to the many friends in the Villages of Melbourne and Seaton Ross for their many deeds of kindness.

'WE SHALL NEVER FORGET'

1/2 October, 1942

In the Autumn of 1942, Bomber Command detailed No.4 Group to attack the U-boat yards at Flensburg. Three attacks were launched over the connecting ten days of September/October but none of the raids appears to have been particularly successful. Of the twenty-eight Halifax bombers that set out on the night of 23/24 September, five were lost and only sixteen aircraft claimed to have bombed the target area. A second raid by twenty-eight Halifaxes three nights later was recalled after take-off, but one aircraft went on to bomb the target and one was lost. The third attempt took place on the night of 1/2 October, 1942, when twenty-seven Halifaxes made the journey across the North Sea.

No.10 Squadron, then based at Melbourne, provided five Halifax Mk IIs for the third attack: W7852/*ZA-K* (piloted by Sergeant KH Meller); DT520/*ZA-J* (Sergeant D Campbell); BB207/*ZA-M* (Pilot Office JL Jones); W7667/*ZA-C* (Sergeant K Hayes); and W1058/*ZA-S* (Sergeant W. Allen).

Squadron Leader Don Hibbert DFC DFM RAF (Ret'd), who was then 'Bill' Allen's rear gunner recalls that:

'Our squadron was detailed to carry out a low-level attack on the U-boat yards. We took off at minute intervals and flew on to Flensburg alone. Bill Allen flew at low level all the way there to avoid detection by German radar.

We were using armour-piercing bombs, the safety height for which was 1,000ft. Because we were going in at low level the bombs had a one-minute delay − to allow us to get away before they exploded. The aircraft were timed to go in at minute intervals, but some arrived early and others were late − and that meant that others had to stooge around out in the Baltic, waiting their turn. As a result, each attacking aircraft was 'expected' and the whole of the town's defences − guns and searchlights − were trained on each aircraft in turn as it made its bombing run.

We went in at 300ft. Although flying at such a height meant that there was no chance of baling out should the need arise, we got low because we believed that would reduce our chances of getting hit. We were so low that their searchlights were *laid down*. Then two searchlights locked on to us; holding us. Don Clay − the mid-upper − couldn't get his guns low enough to shoot at them...

There was *so much* light (20mm) flak ...coloured streams of it floating towards us... coming from all directions. Normally, we didn't *hear* flak: when we did, we knew it was close enough to kill us. Over Flensburg the flak was ripping through the fuselage, making a sound like tearing linen... I was scared to death... I kept my finger on the button all the way across and used over 4,000 rounds in one go. When we came out of it, I had only one gun working — the others had got so hot they'd packed up — but the searchlights had been put out...'

A number of the returning crews reported the severity of the flak defences, which had clearly been strengthened since the previous attacks on the port, and a number of crews reported that those defences alone had accounted for at least four of the Halifaxes lost in the Flensburg area that night. The loss of four aircraft was bad enough — but defenders took their toll both on the way in and on the way out. When the final tally was drawn, the attack of 1/2 October, 1942, had cost No.4 Group twelve (44.4 percent) of the twenty-seven bombers detailed for the raid.

Don Hibbert and his crew were among the lucky ones: when they landed back at base at 01.47hrs the following morning they learned that flak had punched some eighty holes in their aircraft without inflicting injury on any of the occupants. They also learned that they were the sole survivors of the five crews who had set out from Melbourne some

The crew of Halifax MkII W1058/ZA-S at Leeming c. August. 1942. 'Doc' Bullock (wireless operator); Don Clay (mid-upper gunner); Bill Allen (pilot); Don Hibbert (rear gunner); Pete Corfield (bomb aimer); Arthur Lipschitz (navigator); Bill Robinson (flight engineer). On the night of 1/2 October, 1942, the crew were joined by Sergeant GA Vinisg (not shown) who was acting as 2nd pilot.

Three of those shown here were destined not to survive the war: Peter Corfield later fell out of his aircraft without his parachute after a mid-air collision; Arthur Lipschitz, a Czech whose father had died at the hands of the Gestapo , was killed a fortnight after leaving No.10 Squadron and joining No.35 Squadron (Pathfinder Force); and Don Clay was subsequently killed while flying with No.10 Squadron. (Don Hibbert)

Advanced Gunnery Course, RAF Honeybourne, May 1942. This photograph wrongly identifies Don Hibbert as having been killed in June 1942. Don survived the war, but nine of the air gunners in this picture did not. (Don Hibbert)

six hours earlier. Each member was granted an immediate award of the Distinguished Flying Medal.

Of the four crews that were lost, only that of Sergeant Hayes (W7667/*ZA-C*) survived to become prisoners of war; the others were destined never to return. The crews of Sergeant Meller (W7852/*ZA-K*) and Sergeant Jones (BB207/*ZA-M*) now rest in Kiel war cemetery, Germany, while Sergeant Campbell and his crew (D7520/*ZA-J*) lie buried in Odense cemetery, Denmark.

Five nights after the Flensburg raid, No.10 Squadron suffered a loss of almost equal magnitude when it lost three of five Halifaxes despatched to Osnabruck. The fact that half of the Squadron was lost on just two operations gives some indication of the carnage that bomber crews faced in the particularly dangerous years of 1942-1943.

Postscript:

Although the total number of bombs carried to Flensburg by the bombers of No.4 Group that night is not known, No.10 Squadron's contribution was 27 x 1,000lb high-explosives and 900 x 4lb incendiaries. Working on the assumption that the rest of the attacking force were similarly armed, the total number of bombs would have been in the order of 135 x 1,000lbs high-explosives and 4,860 incendiaries.

Twelve of the returning crews claimed to have bombed the target. However, recent examination of the War Damage records at Flensburg Stadtarchiv revealed that only twenty high-explosives and an unspecified number of incendiaries fell on the town. One house was destroyed, and an unspecified number were damaged. Railway lines and water pipes were damaged at the railway station. Total casualties amounted to two killed and one injured.

On the night of 15 October, 1942, Halifax BII W1058/*ZA-S* (No.10 Squadron's sole survivor of the Flensburg operation) was flown to Cologne by another crew: Warrant Officer RK Wildey (pilot); Pilot Officer JW Murphy (2nd pilot); Flight Lieutenant F Davis (navigator); Flight Sergeant A Sanderson-Miller (bomb aimer); Sergeant CE Harrison (wireless operator); Sergeant HD Dubrey (mid-upper gunner); Sergeant HP Burtonshaw (flight engineer); and Flight Lieutenant A Brindley(rear gunner). The aircraft failed to return from that operation.

Squadron Leader Don Hibbert DFC DFM RAF (Ret'd) completed three tours of operations in bombers during the Second World War, two of them with No.4 Group (with No.10 Squadron, Melbourne, and No.158 Squadron, Lissett). He is seen here at the Memorial to No.4 Group RAF and No.6 Group RCAF, which was unveiled at the Yorkshire Air Museum, Elvington, 7 June, 1990.

16/17 September, 1943

The force of 340 bombers which set out on the night of 16/17 September, 1943, to attack the railway yards at Modane, on the French-Italian border, included a No.10 Squadron Halifax B MkIII (JD315/*ZA-R*), based at Melbourne (Yorks). It was crewed by Pilot Officer Jack Heppell (pilot); Flight Sergeant Bill Booth (navigator); Sergeant Stan Adams (bomb aimer); Sergeant Colin Varley (wireless operator); Sergeant Jimmy Grainger (mid-upper gunner); Sergeant Arthur Shaw (flight engineer) and Sergeant Jack Wingate (rear gunner). With the exception of Stan Adams, they had been together for nearly a year, ever since crewing up at No.10 OTU Abingdon; Adams had joined them only the previous month — after their original bomb aimer, Jim Pyne, had decided to seek a change of crew.

On the night of the Modane raid, the original crew of *ZA-R* was further depleted when two members baled out in error. One of those was Bill Booth, whose account of the incident graphically illustrates that wartime fliers faced a multitude of dangers, of which flak and

The crew of No.10 Squadron Halifax JD315/ZA-R after the loss of Bill Booth and Colin Varley on the night of 16/17 September, 1943.
Left to Right: Flying Officer Len Gilding (navigator); Flying Officer Pat Keogh (wireless operator); Pilot Officer Jack Heppell (pilot); Flying Officer Smith (a flight engineer officer who was due to leave the Squadron, having finished his tour); Sergeant Jimmy Grainger (mid-upper gunner); Sergeant Arthur Shaw (flight engineer); Flight Sergeant Stan Adams (bomb aimer); Flight Sergeant Jack Wingate (rear gunner).
Jack Wingate was admitted to hospital on 19 October, 1943. Three nights later the crew went to Kassel, Jack's place being taken by Flight Lieutenant Bill Fagan, Squadron Gunnery Leader, who was on his 76th opperational trip. ZA-R was shot down over the target and the entire crew were killed. (Jack Wingate)

Bill Booth, Flight Sergeant navigator of No.10 Squadron Halifax JD315/ZA-R who baled out in error on the night of 16/17 September, 1943. (Mrs D Booth

Sgt Colin Varley (right) with skipper Jack Heppell c.1942. (C. Varley)

nightfighters constituted only part. An extract from his story is reproduced below with the kind permission of Mrs D Booth and the No.10 Squadron Association.

'We were briefed for a bombing attack on a large railway junction at Modane, on the French-Italian frontier... The target was of great strategic importance at the time because Germany was pouring troops and arms through it from France to hold back our land forces in Italy. The only hazard was the height of the Alpine peaks in the target area. We were instructed to maintain a height of 22,000ft over the Alps to counter this hazard. The weather forecast for the whole of route was clear skies. There was a full moon but as the route was over southern France there was little enemy opposition to be expected. There was every reason to believe that our twentieth operation would be "a piece of cake".

The trip was to be of nine hours' duration so to economize on fuel we were instructed to stay at 10,000ft for the first 100 miles inside France. However, when still about fifty miles short of this position we were confronted by a continuous line of cumulus cloud across our route. The pilot commenced to climb immediately in the hope of getting above it before reaching the Alps, but there was insufficient time. The altimeter registered 18,000ft when we entered the cloud and we were still thousands of feet below the top of it.

Within minutes it became apparent that ice was forming on the plane and as it accumulated the plane quickly lost height until the altimeter registered 15,000ft, when it steadied and felt airborne again. There was plenty of time to reach the required height of 22,000ft: the Alps were about an hour's flying time away and there was always the possibility that the mass of high cloud did not extend that far. However, the skipper decided that he must attempt to get to 22,000ft or above the clouds as soon as possible so with the throttle fully open he tried to climb. Laboriously we reached 18,000ft and then sagged down to about 15,000ft. Three times this happened and each consecutive stall was a little more frightening than the last. The pilot had his intercom switched on, deliberately I think, so we could hear his heavy breathing and occasional grunt as he wrestled with the controls, which were becoming jammed with ice.

This difficulty with the controls had me worried. I had had eight hours' training as a pilot during which time I had practised control of an aircraft in stalls and spins so I knew that there was a strong possibility that we could go into a spin when the plane stalled at 18,000ft. The thought of being in the nose of a spinning Halifax was pretty frightening. There were no safety belts attached to our seats so we could be cut to ribbons. The pilot asked me what I thought we should do... I suggested that we should get down below the cloud and return to base. He did not comment on my suggestion but continued his attempt to climb...

...It seemed an age before what I was expecting happened, but in the light of knowledge gained subsequently it was only about twenty-five minutes after entering the cloud. The plane had again reached a height of 18,000ft when the port wing dipped sharply. 'Bale out, bale out' called the skipper. Then, quickly, 'No, wait,' as the wing lifted. The same wing then dipped even lower and the order came, 'Yes, bale out.'

Knowing that in the event of bale out the wireless operator and the bomb aimer would follow him through the escape hatch positioned below his navigator's station, and in the knowledge that their survival might well depend on the speed at which he freed the hatch, Bill Booth lost no time in jettisoning the door.

'With the removal of the hatch a blast of air came through the aperture, blowing my maps, charts and log from my table, pinning some papers to the sides of my cabin. I sat on the edge of the opening facing the tail-end of the aircraft; my legs dangling through the hole were being pulled strongly by the slip-stream, which was in effect a 200mph wind. A quick glance at Colin, my wireless-operator who was waiting to follow me, then with both hands pushing hard against the opposite side of the opening I slid my backside over the edge and was dragged out by the slip-stream.'

'I was falling through cloud which was just like a dense fog and the sensation of falling was exactly the same as one gets on the big dipper at a fairground, but of course it lasted longer! I was quite calm despite the peculiar feeling in my stomach and groin so I decided to count five instead of the recommended three before pulling the ripcord of my parachute. I made this decision because there was plenty of height to play with and the aircraft was descending rapidly. If the ripcord was pulled too soon there was a possibility of the parachute getting caught up on the tailplane – a horrible thought! I counted a slow five and quickly reached for the ripcord. I used both hands because there was only one ripcord fitted in the end of the parachute pack so, dependent on how it had been clipped on the spring-loaded hooks on the harness, it could be on the left or right-hand side of the pack. Both hands down to my waist level found harness only – no parachute. In a frenzy, my hands went down to my thighs, up to my shoulders, down and up, down and up; there was no parachute there!

I think that I blacked out briefly from sheer terror because when my brain started to function again all sensation of falling was gone. Except for the rush of air which passed me, I could have been lying on the softest of feather beds. I was still in the cloud, which had the appearance of dirty grey cotton wool with the full moon diffusing through it. It was bitterly cold; my face was stiff with frozen tears and I was praying monotonously, 'Oh God. Oh God'. With nothing to see, I could not orient myself. Was I falling head first, feet first? I had no idea but every muscle was tensed against the final impact. Since there was no sensation of falling, I knew that I had reached the terminal velocity for the human body. About 120mph, nearly 200ft per second.

I became calm and strangely reconciled to the fact that I was close to death. I was consoled by the thought that I would not have to face any more operations over heavily defended targets in Germany. I was not going to be burnt in a blazing aircraft – they invariably caught fire when hit by flak or cannon-shell. I was not going to be savagely ripped by jagged splinters of flak – I had made a practice of standing up when over the target to reduce the area of flesh presented to splinters coming up through the floor. 'No,' I thought, 'I won't feel any pain, just a terrific slam and then oblivion'. My parents and close friends would be sad, but they would no longer be waiting for a "Regret" telegram. I had had a good run. I had lost friends on their first operation. The average of five per cent losses on each bombing raid meant statistically that twenty operations was the maximum that a crew could survive. Yes, I was lucky and I was going to die easily and painlessly.

I was still falling through cloud while these thoughts were passing through my head. My body was numb with cold but the air rushing past felt warmer. Suddenly I was out of the cloud and silhouetted against the pale backcloth of the cloud-base, straight in front of my eyes, was a rectangular object, following me because it was attached to my shoulders by webbing.

I realised immediately that it was my parachute and with that knowledge my terror returned. God, had I enough time to get it opened? I had been falling for ages. Which side was the ripcord on? I could not see the ground because, incredibly, I was falling horizontally, face upwards. I had to extend both arms to the limit to reach the pack, a frantic grab at the ends of the pack and although I felt nothing because my hands were numb with cold, there was an immediate flicker of white as the pilot 'chute left the pack, then a mass of white and a savage jerk between my legs as the main 'chute opened. I felt incredibly happy as I hung under the white canopy of silk which I could hear rippling in the wind, but I was crying and shaking like a leaf.

My composure was restored by the sound of aircraft engines, which appeared to be approaching me from above. As I looked up, a Halifax came out of the cloud, nose down and one wing lower than the other. My first thought was that it was out of control and that it was going to pass very close to me. Fear was gripping me again when it became apparent that the pilot had regained control. The wings levelled, the nose lifted. Then, making a tight 150 degree turn, it flew away in a westerly direction...'

Wireless operator Colin Varley had vacated the bomber immediately after Bill Booth – at almost the same time that Heppell countermanded his second order. Bill Booth and Colin Varley were the only members of the crew to bale out. Now, the pilot had regained control: as the parachutists settled earthwards, their aircraft and its crew of five were heading for home. Bill Booth cursed his luck – but Fate would prove to be capricious.

Jack Wingate recalls that when it was realized that Booth and Varley had gone:

'There was a hurried inter-com discussion on what we should do. The options, as I recall, were to bale out over France, to head for

A Halifax BII of No.10 Squadron prepares to touch down at Melbourne. (Mrs C McCoy)

nearby Switzerland and neutrality, or to try to make it back to England.. There was complete agreement that we should have a go at getting back. The skipper now had full control of the aircraft, although some of the instruments were u/s, including the Airspeed Indicator and Artificial Horizon. Fortunately, we soon came out of cloud.

Stan Adams, the bomb-aimer, managed to gather the navigator's maps, which had been blown around with the jettisoning of the escape hatch, and gave an approximate course for southern England. Apart from the obvious tension we were suffering, the journey back over France was uneventful. Skies were clear when we saw the French coast ahead, the problem was: which part of the coast had we reached? A few degrees out in the bomb-aimer's course and we could eventually be heading for a ditching in the North Sea when we ran out of fuel. While Stan was trying to locate our position by map-reading along the coast, we suddenly came under heavy flak attack. Shells were bursting around us and it did not take Stan long to confirm that we were over Cherbourg.. The skipper rapidly set off on a northerly heading, and halfway across the Channel made a Mayday signal. This was rapidly answered with instructions to steer 040 degrees and await the lighting of searchlights. We saw the Isle of Wight, and then two searchlights pointing to what proved to be Tangmere...'

When they eventually got back to Melbourne the five remaining crew members were subsequently joined by replacements Pilot Officer Len Gilding, navigator, and Flying Officer Pat Keogh, wireless operator. Both had already completed a number of operations and thus the crew of *ZA-R* were able to continue as a very experienced team.

They resumed operations flying on 29 September, 1943, when they had to turn back from a raid on Bochum because of low climb performance.

There then followed successful trips to Frankfurt and Hanover, but their luck was not to last.

Jack Wingate remembers that: 'I had for some time been suffering from ear and sinus problems, aggravated by our rapid descent on 16 September, and on the 19 October I was admitted to Station Sick Quarters and later to RAF Hospital, Northallerton...

Flight Sergeant Jack Wingate, rear gunner of No.10 Squadron Halifax JD315/ZA-R, who was admitted to hospital on 19 October, 1943 and thus avoided the fatal crash which occurred three nights later. (J. Wingate)

On 22 October the crew went to Kassel, my place being taken by Flight Lieutenant LWD 'Bill' Fagan, Squadron Gunnery Leader on his seventy-sixth operation. The aircraft was shot down over the target. The entire crew were killed and are buried in the British War Cemetery at Hanover. Ironically, Jim Pyne, who left the crew in August, was lost in HX174/*ZA-H* on the same night with his new crew...'

Postscript:

Bill Booth and Colin Varley landed in the Grenoble area and both were aided by French people willing to risk all for a cause. Some three months later, and by separate routes, they both reached England via Spain. On his return, Bill Booth made enquiries about the cloud conditions in the area where he had baled out. He was informed that on the night of 16/17 September, 1943, the coud base was at 7000ft — '...so my free fall was about 11,000ft duration.'

Both were subsequently transferred to other squadrons and resumed active service. During a later operation, Bill Booth was forced to take to his parachute once more and spent the remainder of the war as a prisoner in Stalag Luft III, of 'Wooden Horse' fame. He died in a car crash in 1980. Colin Varley died in May 1993. Jack Wingate is alive and well and enjoying retirement in the south of England.

Superstition

When I first visited Melbourne, in July 1991, I noticed that a small bouquet of sweet peas had been placed on the monument. The flowers were accompanied by a simple card:

**'In memory of my dear
brother P/O EV Frankland
No. 10 Squadron April 1943
and all other aircrew
who gave their lives'**

Connie

I have since come to know that 'Connie' regularly travels from her native Hull to ensure that the Melbourne stone is always *decorated by a floral tribute, though its precise form does change with the seasons. The written sentiment, however, always remains the same.*

The control tower, Melbourne, January 1992.

The flowers and the card mark the loss of a Halifax and its crew of seven on the night of 4/5 April, 1943. The brief account which follows tells the tale of 'Lofty' Frankland's last operation and points, perhaps, to the fickleness of fate.

On the night of 4/5 April, 1943, Bomber Command launched 577 aircraft against Kiel. One of them was No.10 Squadron Halifax Mk II HR699/ZA-J, crewed by Flying Officer JA Wann (pilot); Flight Sergeant N Bertram (navigator); Sergeant DC Jagger (flight engineer); Sergeant WE Scanlon (air bomber); Sergeant H Wheen (wireless operator); Sergeant Maisenbacher (mid-upper gunner); and Pilot Officer EV Frankland (rear gunner).

Twenty-one year-old 'Lofty' Frankland and his friend 'Boy' Jagger were 'spares' for the Kiel trip. Both normally flew in Flying Officer 'Pitch' Black's Halifax ZA-S, but Black's crew had been temporarily stood down. Len Jewsbury, mid-upper gunner and crewmate of Frankland, remembers:

Sergeant Vernon Frankland, of No.10 Squadron, Melbourne. (Mrs C McCoy)

'We were stood down due to a previous operation, when we had iced-up with a full bomb load and dropped from 13,000ft to 3,000ft in seconds. This, apart from shaking us up a bit, damaged, "Pitch's" ears and he was grounded for eight to nine weeks.

There was no system of automatic allocation of spare crews, but if a crew

Halifax Mk II (L9619) No.10 Squadron, Leeming. This aircraft crashed at Keld, near Shap (Cumbria) on 16 February, 1942, when the crew abandoned it after becoming lost on return from a raid on St. Nazaire (via Lieutenant Colonel R Brousseau)

A flight of Halifax Mk IIs of No.10 Squadron. Vernon Frankland's usual aircraft ZA-S can be clearly seen. He occupied the rear turret on the day the picture was taken. (Mrs C McCoy)

detailed for ops was deficient of a crew-member other aircrew not flying could volunteer or be asked to make up the crew and thus, as put by the senior officers, "make another bomber available for operations". ...Johnny Wann's crew were short of a flight engineer and a rear gunner for the trip to Kiel. Jagger and Frankland were told of this and both agreed to go. It was Lofty's thirteenth trip and Johnny Wann's last (thirtieth) of his tour.'

Aircrew tended to be highly superstitious and many carried their mascots and their lucky charms as safeguards against danger; others had deliberately set patterns in the way they prepared for operations, always exactly the same. Such ritualistic behaviours were rooted in the belief that charms and procedures which had kept crews safe in the past would also keep them safe in the future. Johnny Wann was superstitious, as Len Jewsbury shows:

'It was well known on the Squadron that Johnny Wann always took off first when on ops. This was his own little superstition. He always said: "The first time I don't take off first, I won't return".

However, there was a new crew who were unaware of this superstition of Wann's. They were also detailed for the Kiel raid and, being eager themselves to get off, they beat him to it and he took off second.'

The Kiel raid was not a success: thick cloud obscured the target and strong winds caused difficulties to the Pathfinder unit charged with dropping markers. Few bombs hit the town and none struck industrial or commercial properties.

Melbourne, June 1943. Flying Officer 'Pitch' Black poses with his crew and ground crew in front of their Halifax BIII (ZA-S) (Len Jewsbury)

The attackers lost twelve bombers (and eighty-four aircrew) to flak and to nightfighters, with a further fifteen bombers suffering damage. ZA-J was among those which failed to return. No trace of the aircraft or of its crew has ever been found and it is generally believed that it crashed into the sea.

'Lofty' Frankland and 'Boy' Jagger are commemorated on the Runnymede Memorial: their crewmates on ZA-S survived to see the Peace.

Such is the lottery of war.

No.10 Squadron Memorial, Melbourne, nr York.

OSMOTHERLEY

During January 1944, No.1659 Heavy Conversion Unit, Topcliffe, lost four aircraft in crashes during training. Seventeen aircrew were killed and three were injured as a consequence. Halifax BII LW334 crashed on the morning of 18 January, 1944, when it encountered fog while on a cross-country training flight and struck the northern tip of the Hambleton Hills above Osmotherley, North Yorkshire. Seemingly, the weather had not been good all week: low cloud had hampered flying training and crews had been instructed not to descend below 3,000ft if the ground was not visible. For reasons currently unknown, the bomber was flying at 1,100ft when it impacted, some two hundred feet below the summit of Black Hambleton. There were no survivors.

Fifty years later, the tragedy was commemorated when a simple service was conducted at the site and a wooden cross was dedicated to the memory of the six young Canadians who died in the crash. The initiative for both the service and the cross rest with Cleveland aviation enthusiast and ATC instructor David E Thompson, who had investigated the site on a number of occasions and who had resolved that time should not erase the memory of the incident. He commissioned the cross from Alan Mark of Middlesbrough, approached a local priest to officiate at the dedication, and publicized the service in the local press. At 10.30am Tuesday 18 January, 1994, in a ceremony led by the Reverend Stuart East, parish priest of Upper Rydale, eleven people gathered on the moorland above Osmotherley to honour the memory of six men who had lost their lives thousands of miles from home. Towards the end of the service, a Slingsby Firefly from the Joint Elementary Flying Training School, RAF Topcliffe, made a low pass and dipped its wings in salute.

The wooden cross below Black Hambleton, Osmotherley.
(David E Thompson)

POCKLINGTON

The memorial to No.102 (Ceylon) Squadron and No.405 (Vancouver) Squadron, RCAF, stands alongside the headquarters of the Wolds' Gliding Club on the site of Pocklington's wartime aerodrome. The monument, in the form of a granite column surmounted by an urn, supports a bronze plaque which bears the crests of both squadrons above the inscription:

**ROYAL AIR FORCE
POCKLINGTON AIRFIELD**

**THE HOME OF No.102 (CEYLON) SQUADRON RAF
AND No.405 (VANCOUVER) SQUADRON RCAF No.4
GROUP BOMBER COMMAND DURING WORLD WAR II
FROM WHERE SO MANY GAVE THEIR LIVES IN THE
CAUSE OF FREEDOM.
THIS MEMORIAL WAS RAISED BY OLD COMRADES
TO ALL THOSE MEN AND WOMEN WHO SERVED IN
BOTH SQUADRONS AT THIS AND OTHER BASES IN
WAR AND PEACE.**

The Pocklington memorial stands alongside the HQ of the Wolds' Gliding Club, on the site of the old airfield.

The possibility of erecting a memorial to No.102 (Ceylon) Squadron and to No.405 (Vancouver) Squadron, RCAF, was first suggested to the Town Council by an ex-102 member 'Zeke' Cheffins, of Winnipeg (Canada) who, during a visit to Pocklington, feared that the passing of time would erase all evidence of the site's wartime activities. In June 1983, Pocklington Town Council opened a fund to provide a memorial to both squadrons and the No.102 (Ceylon) Squadron Association launched an appeal in support of that initiative.

Two years later, on 19 May, 1985, the monument was unveiled by Air Chief Marshal Sir Augustus Walker, GCB CBE DSO DFC AFC, a wartime base commander at Pocklington, during a dedication service conducted by Reverend James Woodhouse, Rector of Pocklington, and witnessed by ex-members of both squadrons and a large number of the local population. Lieutenant Colonel KR Allen RCAF, the then Commanding Officer of N0.405 Squadron, travelled from Canada especially for the service and laid a wreath in memory of Squadron members who had failed to return from operations; Wing Commander Stan Craigie laid a wreath in remembrance of No.102 (Ceylon) Squadron members.

The ceremony was concluded by a flypast of a jet Provost of RAF Linton-on-Ouse, a last minute substitution made necessary when the Battle of Britain Memorial Flight had to cancel due to bad weather.

Air Chief Marshal 'Gus' Walker died on 11 December, 1986. The seat that stands alongside the Pocklington memorial carries its own dedication:

IN MEMORY OF
AIR CHIEF MARSHAL SIR AUGUSTUS WALKER
GCB, CBE, DSO, DFC, AFC, MA
BASE COMMANDER OF THE POCKLINGTON BASE
No.4 GROUP, RAF BOMBER COMMAND
JANUARY 1943 until 1945

At the outbreak of war in September 1939, No.102 (Ceylon) Squadron was based at Driffield and was operating with the Whitley Mk III twin-engined bomber, which was replaced two months later by the Mk V version. The Squadron stayed at Driffield until August 1940, when damage inflicted during a daylight attack on the aerodrome by a sizeable force of some thirty Ju88s of KG30 necessitated re-location. On 25 August, 1940, the Squadron moved to Leeming for one week's stay before moving on to Prestwick and then Linton-on-Ouse in quick succession, the average stay being little more that one month at each station.

The move to Topcliffe, on 15 November, 1940, saw the beginning of a more settled period and it was not until exactly one year later that No.102 took up residence at Dalton. The Squadron's conversion to four-engined heavy bombers began with the Halifax Mk II, in December 1941. Six months later, another move took the unit back to Topcliffe for two months before the final war-time move to Pocklington, which had opened in June 1941 as a bomber station in No.4 Group Bomber Command. During its stay at the East Yorkshire base, No.102 Squadron operated two other versions of the Halifax: the Mk III (from May 1944) and the Mk VI (from February 1945).

With the outbreak of hostilities, No.102 Squadron was involved in operational flying right from the start, three of its Whitleys dropping leaflets over the Ruhr on the second night of the war. It served with Bomber Command for the whole of the war, apart from one month spent with Coastal Command in the Autumn of 1940, and carried out its last operation on 25 April, 1945, when eighteen of its Halifaxes bombed gun batteries on the island of Wangerooge. During its period of war service, the Squadron carried out 6,106 sorties in 602 raids at a cost of 192 aircraft (3.1 percent) lost.[1] Awards gained by the Squadron during 1939-45 included five DSOs, one hundred and seventeen DFCs and thirty-four DFMs

On 23 April, 1941, No.405 (Vancouver) Squadron was formed at Driffield, as part of No.4 Group Bomber Command, and was the first Canadian bomber squadron to be established overseas. It was equipped with the Wellington Mk II during the following month and on 20 June it took up residence at Pocklington, which was to be 'home' until August 1942. There then followed a series of rather rapid moves to Topcliffe (7 August, 1942), Beaulieu (25 October, 1942, for a five-month spell with Coastal Command), Topcliffe (1 March, 1943, when the squadron joined the recently formed No.6 (RCAF)Group), and Leeming (6 March, 1943) before making its final move of the war years – to Gransden Lodge(19 April, 1943) as part of No.8 Group (Pathfinder Force). After the move to Pocklington, the Squadron changed aircraft types twice more: in April 1942, when it exchanged its Wellingtons for the Halifax Mk II; and in April, 1943, when it converted to the Lancaster Mk I and Mk III shortly after the move to Gransden Lodge.

During the period of its service with No.4 Group and No.6 (RCAF) Group No.405 squadron carried out 973 sorties in 135 raids at a cost of fifty (5 percent) aircraft lost. Four of those failed to return when No.405 despatched fifteen Halifaxes to Stuttgart on the night of 11/12 March, 1943 – a loss rate of twenty-seven percent. Whilst with No.8 Group

1. Recent evidence suggests that these loss figures understate the case, ignoring as they do non-operational losses and aircraft that crashed in this country on return from operations. Chris Goss, who has been researching aircraft losses for future publication in a history of No.102 (Ceylon) Squadron and who has included all operational and training losses, puts the final figure at 287 aircraft lost and 1,009 personnel killed or missing.

(PFF) the Squadron flew 2,879 sorties on 317 raids Group (PFF) and lost sixty-two (2 percent) aircraft.[2]

Pocklington, 19 May, 1985. Air Chief Marshal Sir Augustus Walker GCB CBE DSO DFC AFC MA flanked by Lieutenant Colonel KR Allen, Canadian Air Force, and Councillor Brian Sellers, Mayor of Pocklington. (Alan Mark via David E Thompson)

2. CASSELS(1991) puts the 405 Squadron losses at higher level. Taking into account non-operational losses and crashes of aircraft in this country upon return from operations (which Bomber Command statistics do not do), he calculates that No.405 Squadron lost 167 aircraft on operations and a further eight in non-operational incidents.

29 March, 1943

On the night of 29 March, 1943, Halifax Mk II (JB848/*DY-G*) of No.102 (Ceylon) Squadron lifted off from its Pocklington base, en route to Berlin. Its crew consisted of Flight Sergeant Bill Comrie (pilot); Flying Officer Douglas Harper (navigator); Pilot Officer Bill Jenkins (bomb aimer); Sergeant 'Jock' McGrath (flight engineer); Sergeant Frank Dorrington (wireless operator); Sergeant John King (mid-upper gunner); and Sergeant Miles Squires (rear gunner).

Five of them had teamed up at No.10 Operational Training Unit, Abingdon, in the last months of 1942; McGrath and King joined them in January 1943, when the quintet transferred to No.102 Heavy Conversion Flight for training on the four-engined Halifax bomber. They graduated to operational flying early in March 1943, at the start of what was to become known as the 'Air Battle of the Ruhr'.

Their first operation took place on 12 March, when Bomber Command despatched 457 aircraft to Essen. Comrie's aircraft was one of ten Halifaxes contributed by Pocklington. The raid cost Bomber Command twenty-three aircraft (5 percent), three of which belonged to No.102 (Ceylon) Squadron (a loss rate of 33.3 percent). Comrie and his crew (in Halifax Mk II HR677) were among the lucky ones: their aircraft

Five of the crew of Halifax Mk II JB848/DY-G of No.102 (Ceylon) Squadron who perished when their aircraft crashed at Pocklington's West Green, 29 March 1943. L to R: Sergeant Miles Squires (rear gunner); Flying Officer Douglas Harper (navigator); Flight Sergeant Bill Comrie (pilot); Sergeant Frank Dorrington (wireless operator); Pilot Officer Bill Jenkins (bomb aimer). (S. Harper via C. Stokoe)

sustained only small flak holes in the fuselage, none of which caused serious difficulties.

Their second trip took place on 26 March, 1943, when they went to Duisberg as part of a force of 455 bombers. Bomber Command escaped lightly on that occasion, only six aircraft (1.3 percent) failing to return. No.102 Squadron's contribution to the raiding force was thirteen — a number with which to tempt fate, perhaps, but all managed the return trip. Again, Bill Comrie and his crew (in Halifax JB848/*DY-G*) were lucky, but they did not escape scot free: subsequent examination of the aircraft showed a small hole in the port wing and a hole in the starboard outer oil tank.

Their third operation would have taken them to Berlin on 29 March, 1943. 329 aircraft were detailed for the trip and twenty-one (6.4 percent) of those would be lost over occupied Europe. Comrie and his crew were scheduled for the operation but they never got beyond Pocklington, because their luck ran out shortly after they lifted off from the tarmac.

In 1943 there were some twenty-seven airfields and landing grounds in Yorkshire. They were concentrated in a rough 'L' shape, which stretched southwards from the river Tees to York and then eastwards towards the coast. A number of these airfields were so close to each other that they shared common landing and take-off circuits, a situation that offered potential dangers when many aircraft were preparing to land or to take off. Pocklington shared a common circuit with the nearby aerodromes of Melbourne and Elvington — and 29 March, 1943 was a busy night.

The poor weather conditions — cloud and intermittent rain — ensured that the starting time of the Berlin operation was postponed twice from the 7.00pm originally planned. The first of Pocklington's Halifaxes finally got under way at 21.45hrs: Comrie's aircraft lifted off thirteen minutes later — with a full load of high-explosives, incendiary bombs and some 2,000 gallons of fuel.

There is some speculation with regard to what happened next but it is believed that when *G-George* cleared cloud a minute or so later it was very close to another aircraft. Whether that second aircraft got under the wing of *G-George* and thus caused the Halifax to flip over, or whether Comrie's attempt at evasive action caused his bomber to stall and then invert, might never be known. However, according to a number of ground-based witnesses, Comrie's aircraft *was upside down* when it fell to earth. With virtually no height to recover, the fully-laden bomber plunged into a field opposite Pocklington School, the detonation on impact being sufficiently loud to be heard five miles away at Melbourne. All seven members of the crew were killed.

Halifax Mk III (DY-E), No.102 Squadron, Pocklington, c.1943 (Stan Jefferey)

23 August, 1943.

The dangers faced by bomber crews were not restricted to flights over continental Europe. Just taking off from the home base could bring its own tensions. As an ex-195 Squadron rear gunner once pointed out to me:

> 'Two thousand gallons of fuel and six tons of bombs − and you're sitting on that as you go thundering down the runway, hoping that you'll get up all right.'

When some did not, the consequences were often dire. But sometimes Fate smiled more generously. Such was the case with Wing Commander Stanley Marchbank and the crew of Halifax Mk II JD127/*DY-U*, of No.102 (Ceylon) Squadron, Pocklington, one night in 1943.

On 23 August, 1943, Bomber Command sent 727 bombers against Berlin and lost fifty-six (7.7 percent). No.102 (Ceylon) Squadron's contribution *was to have* been twenty-three Halifaxes, but only fourteen made the trip because the fifteenth crashed on take-off and in so doing it blocked the runway. Marchbank's Halifax *was* the fifteenth and when it failed to lift off it had a full fuel load and some 4,000lbs of bombs on board. Fifty years later, Stanley Marchbank recalled the incident:

> 'At Pocklington, one of the runways ran within the danger zone of the flying control tower and, therefore, a deep trench had been dug in front of it, the purpose of which was to wipe the undercarriage off any errant aircraft...
>
> On take off, I opened up the throttles and almost immediately power decreased on the port side. Try as I might I could not correct the swing; in no time at all one wheel was on the grass and we were heading for the control tower...'

But then the trench intervened.

'...Off came the undercarriage and the aircraft slithered to halt not far short of the building. I seem to remember that under the cicumstances – and I hope that I am correct! – the first chap out had to be the pilot, through the escape hatch in the top of the cockpit. The rest of my crew followed very smartly. The aircraft was on fire and we all high-tailed it across the airfield as fast as we could. At some stage we threw ourselves on to the ground and waited for the big bang... When the inevitable happened... innumerable windows were removed, and no good was done to the buildings – in particular the control tower. Those inside had exited in no time at all, the roly-poly base navigation officer through a window – and, try as he might, he never did succeed in repeating the feat! We were not seen to get out of the aircraft and were given up for dead. When we wandered back across the airfield and turned up out of the gloom people were astonished... Two things saved us: the ditch and well-practised and disciplined escape drill...'

Not all 102 Squadron's crews had such luck that night. Halifax Mk II JD407/*DY-R*, piloted by Sergeant GS Roadley, took off for Berlin at 8.26pm and never returned.

Wing Commander Stanley Marchbank (in cockpit) and his crew, who had a lucky escape at Pocklington on the night of 24 August 1943. (via Chris Goss)

29 January, 1944.

677 bomber aircraft took part in the raid on Berlin on the night of 28/29 January 1944: forty-six (6.8 percent) failed to return. Many fell victim to the concentration of nightfighters in the vicinity of the target — but a Pocklington-based Halifax Mk II (JD165/DY-S) was caught by flak as it left the target area: shrapnel damaged the rudder controls and holed two fuel tanks in the starboard wing. The damage sustained to the rudder controls subsequently proved to be repairable; the loss of fuel from the punctured tanks could not be remedied. The crew managed to nurse the bomber to the Danish coast and out over the North Sea, but the steady loss of fuel meant that there was virtually no chance of reaching England.

At 09.00hrs on 29 January, 1944, when they were some eighty miles east of Dundee, their luck ran out and pilot Flight Sergeant DM Pugh had to ditch his aircraft in a 'very rough sea' — but not before the SOS transmitted by Sergeant A Cohen (wireless operator) had been acknowledged.

The crew took to their dinghy without difficulty but the cruel cold soon took its toll, numbing fingers and thus making it impossible for the fliers to use their sealed rations. A bad situation was made very much worse a short time later when a large wave capsized the dinghy and cast its occupants into the chilling water. Only Flight Sergeant Pugh, Sergeant Cohen, Sergeant C Williams (air gunner), and Flight Sergeant J Graham

The churchyard of St Catherine's, Barmby Moor, nr Pocklington, contains the graves of fifty-four airmen: twenty-seven RAF; twenty-two RCAF, three RNZAF and two RAAF.

Flight Sergeant DM Pugh, pilot of No.102 Squadron Halifax JD165/DY-S, who survived three days adrift in the North Sea in January 1944. (via Chris Goss)

(navigator) were able to struggle back into the rubber boat. Sergeant A Burgess (air gunner), Sergeant R Purkiss (flight engineer) and Sergeant E Campbell (bomb aimer), beaten by the cold and by the strength-sapping weight of water-logged clothing, could not manage it. Even though their four crew mates made what efforts they could to pull them aboard, it was to no avail: the trio could only float alongside, their numbed fingers attempting to clutch dinghy lifelines. Eventually, each lost his hold on life and drifted silently away.

The four survivors were adrift for some thirty-six hours before they were first spotted by an Air-Sea Rescue (ASR) search aircraft, which did drop survival aids to them – but the rough seas made retrieval impossible. When the four were found again by an ASR aircraft they were into their third day at sea and in very bad shape. However, the aircraft was able to direct an ASR launch to the scene and the fliers were finally picked up on 1 February and taken to RAF Montrose. Sad to say, for Sergeant Graham, who had endured so much in the most extreme circumstances, rescue came just a little too late: he died whilst enroute to harbour; his crewmates lived to tell the tale.

'T2' Type hangar at Pocklington, October 1993

'K' Type hangar at Pocklington, October 1993

SELBY

At the outbreak of war, No.51 Squadron was equipped with Whitley III twin-engined bombers and was based at Linton-on-Ouse. The Squadron changed to Whitley IVs in November and then to Whitley Vs in January, 1940, one month after moving to Dishforth. It stayed there until 6 May, 1942, when it moved south to Chivenor (Devon) for a five-month spell with Coastal Command before returning north, to Snaith, on 27 October. In the following month the Squadron converted to Halifax IIs and later — January 1944 — to Halifax IIIs, which it continued to use until the end of the war.

No.51 was already operational when hostilities broke out and it flew the first sortie of the conflict when three of its aircraft dropped leaflets over Hamburg on the night of 3 September 1939. It helped to pioneer airborne assault operations when it flew paratroops on the first such raid — the attack on the Tragino (Southern Italy) viaduct on 10/11 February, 1941. It also flew parachute forces on the Bruneval raid of 27/28 February, 1942.

The Squadron participated in all of the major air operations of the Second World War. It flew 5,959 sorties in 497 raids and lost 158 (2.7 percent) aircraft.[1]

The granite memorial which was unveiled on 9 June, 1984, 'in proud and undying memory of all ranks killed or missing 1939– 1945' is located in the Abbey grounds, Selby, some ten miles north of Snaith. This was felt to be a more appropriate location than the old airfield, largely because the aerodrome is off the beaten track and is also gradually being converted to industrial use. In addition, wartime crews operating from Snaith came to regard Selby as their 'home' and thus it seemed proper that the memorial should be placed in the Abbey grounds. Some 400 Association members and their families, as well as local dignitaries and serving members of No.51 Squadron attended the service.

No.51 Squadron memorial is located in the grounds of Selby Abbey.

Snaith airfield, March 1994

The monument was dedicated by the serving Station Chaplain of RAF Wyton, No.51 Squadron's base in 1984, at a service conducted by the Rev. Michael Escritt (Vicar of Selby Abbey), and the Roman Catholic Chaplain at RAF Wyton, Father Paul Richmond. The flypast was provided by a No.51 Squadron Nimrod, which made two passes over the Abbey.

After the unveiling of the Selby memorial to No.51 Squadron, 9 June, 1984. L to R: AK Dean DFC (4th); Air Commodore BN Speed (8th); Group Captain DH Barnes OBE (9th); Wing Commander EW Tyzack, OC No.51 Squadron (10th); J Fever DFC (11th); J Gill AFM (12th). (via Jim Fever)

1. K. FORD(1993) gives the total loss figures as ninety-two Whitleys, 168 Halifaxes, 920 personnel killed (including 211 who lost their lives in Whitley crashes, and ten ground crew who were killed in a bomb dump explosion). Some 394 decorations were awarded to Squadron members.

30/31 March, 1944

On the night of 30/31 March, 1944, Bomber Command launched 795 aircraft against Nuremberg. It cost them dearly: ninety-five (11.9 percent) bombers were lost and a further seventy-one were damaged, eleven so badly that they were beyond repair.

A Bomber Command report of the operation highlights the reasons:

'German nightfighters, who had considerable success and

accounted for most of the losses, were to some extent helped by the weather. The strong north-westerly wind that had been forecast proved to be both weaker and less northerly than expected. Thus the bombers were soon extended over a broad belt to the north of track. In addition, the cloud which had been expected to cover the bombers, at least over the first part of the route, dispersed altogether beyond Belgium and left the attacking force exposed in bright moonlight.

German fighter controllers discounted the idea of a serious threat from the north, where some fifty Halifaxes were laying mines in Heligoland Bight, and massed their fighters in two groups near Bonn and Frankfurt, from where they easily intercepted the bomber stream. A running battle then developed over a distance of some 250 miles, from Aachen eastwards and then southwards to the target.

Nightfighters destroyed at least fifty bombers between Aachen

No.51 Squadron Halifax HR868/MH-B after its encounter with a nightfighter while enroute to Frankfurt on the night of 20 December, 1943. Examination of the aircraft after landing showed that the port elevator was completely shattered, the trimming controls and the rear part of the fuselage were riddled with bullet holes. Two cannon shells had burst in the nacelle of the port engine and there was extensive damage to the main spar web and boom. A cannon shell had also burst in the nose and another had gone through the bomb doors, setting fire to incendiaries stored there. In addition, the bomb door hydraulic pipe line was severed and the petrol line was affected. The pilot got the plane back to Snaith, where he put it down safely in spite of a burst tyre. (Imperial War Museum CE114)

Halifax crews of No.51 Squadron, Snaith, are briefed for the attack on Nuremberg which took place on the night of 30/31 March, 1944. Of the 795 aircraft despatched by Bomber Command, 95 (11.9%) failed to return. No.51 Squadron lost six (35.3%) of the seventeen aircraft it sent on the raid. Thirty-five of the men who attended this briefing were killed; seven more became prisoners of war. (IWM 12598)

and the turning point near Fulda (north-east of Frankfurt); three on the southerly run in; five over the target; and four on the way home. Flak accounted for fourteen aircraft, according to observations recorded by aircrew: at Namur, Aachen, Bonn (two), Coblenz, Schweinfurt (two), Strasbourg, Le Touquet and Nuremberg (five); two collided over the target and were seen to go down in flames.'

No.51 Squadron, Snaith lost six (35.3 percent) of the seventeen Halifaxes it despatched: five over Germany and one in England. Of the five that fell over Germany, four were the victims of night-fighters: LV822/*MH-Z* (piloted by Flight Sergeant E Wilkins) crashed near Helborn with no survivors among the seven-man crew; LW544/*MH-Q* (Sergeant GC Brougham) was cut down north-west of Alsfeld with a loss of five of the crew; LV857/*MH-H* (Sergeant JPG Pinder) was lost with its entire crew noth-east of Fulda; and LW537/*MH-C* (Flight Sergeant Stembridge) was shot down to the east of Fulda with the loss of two crew. The fifth

Halifax (LV777/*MH-E*) succumbed to flak over Stuttgart: its pilot, Squadron Leader FP Hill, was on the 13th trip of his tour. The sixth Halifax made its way back to England.

Halifax Mk III LW579/*MH-V* was crewed by Pilot Officer J Brooks (pilot); Flight Sergeant DP McCormack (navigator); Sergeant RF Kelly (bomb aimer); Sergeant TS Connell (flight engineer); Flight Sergeant GW West (wireless operator); Sergeant DA Churchill (mid-upper gunner); and Sergeant S Glass (rear gunner). Sergeant Kelly was a 'spare': the regular bomb aimer, Flying Officer K King, had been excused from the Nuremberg trip because of an attack of shingles.

Prior to Nuremberg, this experienced crew had survived − almost without incident − nineteen operations on which a total of 529 heavy bombers had been lost. But on the night of 30/31 March, 1944, it was *their* turn. Unlike ninety-four other crews, the men in *MH-V* did survive the carnage of the Nuremberg trip, but a safe return to base was to be denied them.

It is not known whether the Halifax had sustained battle-damage during the raid, but seven hours and thirteen minutes after leaving Snaith Brooks was heading for an emergency landing at RAF Benson, Oxfordshire. Eye-witnesses claim that as the Halifax made its approach, all four engines were running and the undercarriage was lowered.

It was dark and the cloud was down − low enough to enshroud the wooded summit of a 900ft hill that lay across the path of the bomber. It is a matter of conjecture whether Brooks was unaware of the high ground that lay ahead or whether his aircraft had sustained damage which made evasive action impossible. What is not in doubt is that the trees on the summit caught the bomber's undercarriage and dragged the aircraft to earth. It crashed at 5.20am in Cowlease Wood, Stokenchurch, and exploded on impact. There were no survivors.

Flight Sergeant George William West, wireless-operator of Halifax Mk III LW579/MH-V, No.51 Squadron, Snaith. (D. Sholl)

No.51 Squadron lost forty-two aircrew on that night: thirty-five were killed and seven became prisoners of war. Flying Officer King, saved from the Nuremberg trip by an attack of shingles, survived the war: he died in 1976.

Postscript:

On 31 March, 1994, the fiftieth anniversary of the crash, some 130 people gathered at the site to witness the unveiling of a small granite memorial to the crew. The ceremony was the culmination of the efforts of Dennis Churchill (son of Flight Sergeant DA Churchill) and David Sholl (nephew of Flight Sergeant GW West) to ensure that such sacrifices should not be forgotten.

Record of operations undertaken by Pilot Officer Brook's crew: No.51 Squadron, Snaith.[1]

Date	Target	Aircraft	Number	Aircraft desp.	lost	%
17 Aug 43	PEENEMUNDE	Halfx. II	HR946	596	40	6.7
23 Aug 43	BERLIN	Halfx. II	JD308	727	56	7.7
[Abandoned op; unable to gain height]						
31 Aug 43	BERLIN	Halfx. II	JN885	622	47	7.6
23 Aug 43	MANNHEIM	Halfx. II	JN885	628	32	5.1
27 Sep 43	HANOVER	Halfx. II	HR949	678	38	5.6
2 Oct 43	MINELAYING	Halfx. II	HR949		-	
11 Nov 43	CANNES	Halfx. II	HR782	124	4	3.2
18 Nov 43	MANNHEIM	Halfx. II	HR782	395	23	5.8
20 Dec 43	FRANKFURT	Halfx. II	HR949	650	41	6.3
[Abandoned op; unable to gain height]						
29 Dec	BERLIN	Halfx. II	JD461	712	20	2.8
24 Feb 44	SCHWEINFURT	Halfx. II	LW498	734	33	4.5
25 Feb 44	AUGSBURG	Halfx. III	LW504	594	21	3.5
[Abandoned op; technical problems]						
7 Mar 44	LE MANS	Halfx. II	LW541	304	nil	-
13 Mar 44	LE MANS	Halfx. III	LW504	213	1	0.4
15 Mar 44	STUTTGART	Halfx. III	LW504	863	37	4.3
18 Mar 44	FRANKFURT	Halfx. III	LW504	846	22	2.6
22 Mar 44	FRANKFURT	Halfx. III	LW504	816	33	4.0
24 Mar 44	BERLIN	Halfx. III	LW504	811	72	8.9
26 Mar 44	ESSEN	Halfx. III	LW504	705	9	1.3
30 Mar 44	NUREMBERG	Halfx. III	LW579	795	95	11.9

[Crashed at Stokenchurch, Oxford, on return from Nuremberg. All crew killed]

[1] [Based on information provided by David Sholl and from *Bomber Command War Diaries*, 1990 ed]

13 January, 1945

There were times when aircrews survived the flak and attacks by night-fighters only to die as the consequence of a tragic accident. One such occurrence took place on the night of 13 January, 1945, when Halifax

The original crew of Halifax MkIIILW579/MH-V, No.51 Squadron, Snaith. **Back row (L to R):** *Sergeant TS Connell (flight engineer); Flight Sergeant GW West (wireless operator); Flight Sergeant DP McCormack (navigator); Sergeant DA Churchill (mid-upper gunner).* **Front row (L to R):** *Flight Sergeant S Glass (rear gunner); Flying Officer K King (bomb aimer); Sergeant (later Pilot Officer) J Brookes (pilot).*
Because of an attack of shingles, Flying Officer King missed the Nuremberg raid. His place was taken by Sergeant S Kelly, whose regular pilot was ill. King was destined to be the only member of his crew to survive the war: he died in 1976. (David Sholl)

Mk III *MX465/MH-Y* (No.51 Squadron, Snaith) was returning from Saarbrucken at the same time as an Elvington-based Halifax (No.LL590) of No.347 (Tunisie) Squadron. For reasons currently unknown, the two aircraft collided. The tail fin of the Free French aircraft severed the nose of *MH-Y* and cast the navigator (Sergeant H Whitehouse) and bomb aimer (Flight Sergeant D Hauber) into the night. Neither was wearing a parachute. In spite of the damage to his aircraft, Wilson managed to return to Snaith. The fate of the French crew is not known.

TINGLEY

The monument in Yorkshire stone that stands alongside the main Bradford-Wakefield road (A.650) at Tingley commemorates the seven crew members of a Mk III Halifax bomber who died when their aircraft crashed in a nearby field on 14 November, 1944.

(*Walter Townend*)

The 51 Squadron Halifax (LK844/MH-M) had taken off from its base at Snaith at 5.22pm to carry out a night cross-country exercise. Eight minutes later, in conditions of failing light, low cloud and falling rain, it exploded over Tingley before crashing in a field off Thorpe Lane.

Debris was scattered 'over a very large area' and several houses were damaged, including that of Sidney Knight, a shunter who was at work at the Thorpe Lane Railway Goods Yard. He and a number of colleagues had suspected that something was amiss as the bomber circled over their workplace. Knight later recalled that: '... all those at the Goods Yard thought that it would crash on the railway line...' In fact, it demolished the upper storey of his house – without causing injury to his wife and three-year-old daughter who were in the kitchen below.

The seven crew members – Flight Sergeant CW Millard (pilot); Sergeant VT Spragg (navigator); Sergeant AF Simpson (bomb aimer); Sergeant WP Kendrick (flight engineer); Sergeant John Hill (wireless operator); Sergeant AW Payton (mid-upper gunner); and Sergeant KD

121

Saines (rear gunner) — were destined not to survive. Two members did manage to take to their parachutes, but it is believed that they were killed by the blast from the explosion as they glided earthwards.

It seems unlikely that the actual cause of the crash will ever been known. Eye-witnesses reported the aircraft's '...semi-circular direction of flight prior to the crash and that before the explosion the aircraft began to jettison some of its equipment, which was found over a large area...' The Air Investigation Branch *assumed* that control had been lost due to bad weather, ice being suggested as a possible contributory factor.

Walter Townend, now of Leeds, witnessed the crash as a thirteen year old schoolboy and never forgot the incident that made him appreciate for the first time '...the reality and the tragedy of war...'. In January 1988, he started to research the crash for a personal scrapbook. It was during the course of that investigation that he realized that the passing of time would inevitably ensure '...fewer people would remember that tragic piece of village history...' He felt that there should be a public reminder of the crew's sacrifice and thus he resolved to erect a commemorative stone at his own expense.

The Tingley monument was dedicated on Sunday, 12 November, 1989, during a service conducted by the Vicar of Woodkirk, the Reverend Terry King, and attended by Mervyn Rees MP, twenty-four relatives of the crew, and representatives from No.51 Squadron. The stone was unveiled by two ex-No.51 Squadron members, 'Ricky' Pearce (Market Weighton) and George Booth (Stoke-on-Trent), who had flown twenty-one operations in LK844 after it was assigned to the Squadron in April 1944.

The house of Sidney Knight after it had been struck by debris from Halifax LK844/MH-M

SELBY

The plaque that hangs in the Church of St James the Apostle, Selby, commemorates those who lost their lives in 1944 when a Halifax bomber struck the church spire.

(Reverend Margaret Cundiff)

On the night of 9/10 May, 1944, Halifax bomber JB798, of 1658 Heavy Conversion Unit, Riccall (near Selby), was participating in a night-flying exercise. The seven members of the crew consisted of: Flight Sergeant Thomas Laver (pilot); Sergeant Derrick McDermott (flight engineer); Sergeant Hillary Rockingham (navigator); Flight Sergeant Noel Knight (wireless operator); Sergeant Bernard Storer (bomb-aimer); Flying Officer John Dixon (air gunner); and Sergeant John Roper (air gunner). Five of them were Australians and two — McDermott and Rockingham — were British.

Laver had already completed some ninety minutes of dual instruction that night before he was allowed to go solo for a series of 'circuits and bumps'. He had just completed his third successive landing of the exercise and the Halifax was climbing away to the south when observers on the aerodrome runway thought they caught a glimpse of fire. Subsequent attempts by Control to warn Laver via the radio link were to no avail as the bomber flew off at low altitude towards Selby, some three miles to the south.

Laver approached the town at an altitude a little in excess of one hundred feet, but the reason for his lack of height has never been satisfactorily established, partly because the evidence offered by eye-witnesses was contradictory. For example, only the Riccall observers made reference to the possibility of the aircraft being on fire, while there was also similar confusion regarding possible mechanical problems. Eye-witness Arthur Hall claimed that the aircraft was in distress and that its engines were '...making a peculiar noise and its wings were waggling up and down..' just before it crashed (*Selby Times* 12 May, 1944). However, Hall's claim was subsequently disputed by a number of witnesses who claimed that the plane was flying normally prior to impact (*Selby Times* 19 May, 1944).

Whatever the reason for the bomber's lack of altitude, all witnesses were agreed that it was too low. In fact, it was the plane's height that spurred Police Reserve Constable Lawrence Clayton to action *before* disaster struck. He was on duty near Selby's Brook Street telephone kiosk when he saw the plane:

'It was flying on a perfectly even keel but it was making a direct line for St. James's Church and so certain was I that it was going to crash that I ran to the phone box. At that point it hit the centre of the steeple and burst into flames. The flames seemed to run along for three or four hundred yards and there was another big crash and a burst of flames' (*Selby Times* 19 May, 1944)

The bomber sliced 30ft off the top of the 140ft spire before it careered into the back gardens of Portholme Drive, where two houses (nos 30 and 32) were reduced to flaming debris and a third (no.34) was set ablaze. The crew and eight civilians were killed, including four of the five members of the Osbourn family. The average age of the crew was 21 years.

St James Church, Selby, before the collision...and after

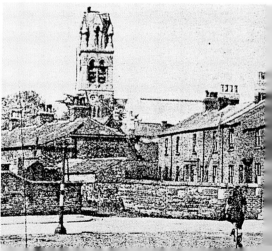

WETHERBY

In May 1992, members of the Wetherby Golf Club erected a memorial stone on the exact spot where a Halifax bomber crashed on their golf course forty-eight years earlier.

On 24 August, 1944, a Halifax Mk II (DG226) of 1652 Heavy Conversion Unit took off from Marston Moor at 2.20pm on a training flight. Eye-witnesses saw it flying in a north-westerly direction as it climbed over Wetherby. When the aircraft was at 1,000ft, smoke began to pour from the port outer engine shortly before the Halifax banked and rapidly began to lose height. The six members of the crew had no time to bale out and all were killed when their aircraft inverted and dived into the ground between the river and the railway, some one

29 May 1992. Wing Commander Bobby Sage, President of the Yorkshire Air Museum, Elvington, unveils the Wetherby memorial. (Yorkshire Post)

hundred yards from the clubhouse. Burning wreckage was strewn over surrounding fields and although a number of golfers were on the course at the time, none was injured.

The members of the crews who died were as follows:

Flight Sergeant C.R. Osbourne RCAF(pilot)
Sergeant G.E. Robinson RAF (flight engineer)
Sergeant E.G. Barrie RCAF(navigator)
Flying Officer G.D. Burnie RCAF(bomb aimer)
Flying Officer H. Jones RAF (wireless operator)
Flight Sergeant J.D. Morrison RCAF(air gunner)

The Canadians were buried in Stonefall cemetery, Harrogate; it is believed that the British members of the crew were buried in their home towns.

RAF investigators recovered the port outer engine and subsequent examination revealed a broken con rod, which had caused the engine to seize up. However, whether that was the cause of the crash might well be a matter of conjecture for a Halifax in capable hands could be flown quite easily on three engines or even fewer.

In 1976, a 'dig' led by Leeds-based Nick Roberts unearthed a substantial amount of wreckage, including: two 10lb bombs, a packed parachute, the starboard wing, a complete undercarriage, engine

Wetherby resident Colin Harvey, who witnessed the crash of Halifax DG226 in 1944, inspects one of the engines excavated from the site in May 1992. (Yorkshire Post)

cowlings and both starboard engines. The starboard outer was later taken to Yorkshire Air Museum, Elvington, for display; the starboard inner was retained by farmer Hubert Robinson, on whose land the wreck lay buried and who as a young boy had witnessed the crash in 1944. The port inner engine was excavated during the week commencing 25 May, 1992.

The memorial was unveiled on Friday, 29 May, 1992, by Wing Commander Bobby Sage, President of the Yorkshire Air Museum, Elvington, in the presence of representatives from the RCAF, the RAF, Wetherby Council and members of Wetherby Golf Club during a short service conducted by the Reverend Norman Berryman, chaplain to the Yorkshire Air Museum. The local Air Taining Corps Squadron provided the guard of honour and a flypast was provided by a single Tornado, which performed a slow roll in salute.

No.431 (Iroquois) Squadron and
No.434 (Bluenose) Squadron, RCAF

DALTON-ON-TEES

Some four miles south of Darlington, the A167 skirts the small community
of Dalton-on-Tees. On the swathe of green at the south end of the village
the sculptured figure of an airman stands on a plinth of Cornish granite.
Dressed in full flying kit and with a parachute pack at his feet, he casts
an eye skywards, his left arm raised to obstruct the sun's glare.

The RCAF memorial, Dalton-on-Tees.

The monument is a testament to the men of the Royal Canadian Air Force who flew from nearby Croft aerodrome during the Second World War. Appropriately, the figure overlooks the approach to what was once the main runway

The true cost of this memorial, as with all such reminders of War's penalties, was met in another time and another place, but the financial charge was paid in Canada by ex-members of No.431 (Iroquois) Squadron and No.434 (Bluenose) Squadron who operated from the aerodrome from December, 1943 until June, 1945.

No.431 Squadron was formed at Burn on 13 November, 1942, and operated with the Wellington Mk Xs until moving to Tholthorpe on 15 July, 1943. They became a heavy bomber squadron during the same month, when they re-equipped with the Halifax Mk V. The Squadron took up residence at Croft in the second week of December 1943 and stayed there until departing for Canada in June 1945. While at Croft they changed aircraft type twice, converting to the Halifax Mk III in March 1944 and to the Lancaster Mk X in the following October.

No.434 Squadron was formed at Tholthorpe on 15 June, 1943, and initially operated the Halifax Mk V, a type which it took to Croft when the Squadron was posted there six months later. No. 434 stayed at the Co. Durham base until June 1945 and − like No.431 − they changed aircraft type twice : to the Halifax Mk III in May 1944; the Lancaster Mk X in December 1944. They also flew the Lancaster Mk I and Mk III alongside the Mk X from February to March 1945.

During the Second World War, the fortunes of those two bomber squadrons bore striking similarities whilst they were based at Croft: they arrived together in '43 and left together in '45; they flew the same types of aircraft and shared the same operations; they flew almost the same number of sorties (2,578 by No.431 Squadron; 2,597 by No.434 Squadron), lost the same number of aircraft (seventy-five by No.431 Squadron; seventy-five by No.434 Squadron)[1] and suffered virtually identical casualties (No.431 Squadron lost 504 personnel, including fourteen in non-operational incidents, of which 381 were killed or presumed dead; and No.434 Squadron lost 493, of which 358 were killed or presumed dead).

In eighteen months of operations the combined total of losses was 969 aircrew, 725 of whom were killed or presumed dead; the remainder became prisoners of war or made good their escape. In effect, these losses represented each squadron being wiped out twice in year and half!

Representatives of both Squadron Associations wanted a monument to such sacrifice to be erected on site. They approached Peter Simpson, then Chairman of Dalton-on-Tees Parish Council, who enlisted the support of local plumber, Alec Clacher. In collaboration with Tholthorpe farmer Geoff Wood and York-based Squadron Leader Jim Cable and his wife they became the 'driving force' at the British end of the project and worked in close collaboration with their Canadian counterparts.

Their efforts came to fruition on Saturday, 26 September, 1987, when the monument was unveiled by RCAF Brigadier-General 'Bill' Newson, DSO DFC (who commanded No.431 Squadron during its time at Croft) and was dedicated by the Dean of York, the Very Reverend John Southgate. A parade of some 250 veterans, followed by a contingent from the RAF Regiment, Catterick, preceded the ceremony. In a fitting climax, a flypast by the Lancaster bomber of the RAF Memorial Flight brought the ceremony to a dramatic and emotional conclusion for many of the veterans who were present.

Inscription:

Per Adua Ad Astra

**In memory of
and to honour
those who served
at Croft during
World War II.
Dedicated by the
Members of 431 Iroquois
and 434 Bluenose
RCAF Squadrons
6 Group Bomber Command
26 September 1987**

**78 Squadron RAF 1664 HCU
419 427 431 434 Squadrons RCAF
1941 − 1945**

---

1. HALPENNY(1982) states that 431 Squadron flew 2573 sorties for 72 aircraft lost; he agrees the number of sorties flown by 434 Squadron but gives aircraft losses as 74.

August 1943 – February 1944

Some indication of the dangers faced by bomber crews, particularly in the 1943-44 period, is highlighted by the experience of No.434 (Bluenose) Squadron, which formed at Tholthorpe on 15 June, 1943. Most of its casualties were sustained during the first six months of operations, from August 1943 to February 1944, when forty-three crews (313 men) failed to return from operations. This represents an average casualty rate of 11.8 per cent over 364 sorties.

The Squadron carried out its first operation on 12 August, 1943, when nine Halifaxes bombed Milan and returned safely to Tholthorpe. Five days later, Bomber Command sent 596 aircraft to attack the V1/V2 experimental rocket station at Peenemunde and lost forty (6.7 per cent) of them. No.434 Squadron's contribution was ten Halifaxes, of which three (33 per cent) failed to return. Between 22 August and 6 September, 1943, the Squadron attacked some of the most heavily defended targets in Germany, including Berlin and Nuremberg, at a cost of six aircraft (and forty-two aircrew) lost. Operations conducted during the period 15 September to 3 December, 1943, cost another twenty aircraft (and 140 aircrew). This represented an average loss rate of 11 per cent per operation during the last four months of 1943. However, this average was surpassed on the night of 22/23 October of that year when Bomber Command sent 569 aircraft to Kassel and lost forty-three (7.6 per cent): No.434 Squadron despatched twelve Halifaxes to Kassel; four (33 per cent) of them failed to return.

The Squadron took up residence at Croft on 11 December, 1943. Over the following two months they carried out seven operations and lost sixteen (19.5 per cent)of the eighty-two aircraft despatched. Five of those were lost on the Berlin raid on the night of 28/29 January, 1944. Bomber Command sent 677 aircraft against the 'Big City', forty-six (6.8 per cent) of which did not return; No.434 (Bluenose) Squadron despatched twelve – and lost forty-two per cent of them.[1]

1. **Squadron statistics from** *No.434 Squadron History* (1984); Bomber Command details from *Bomber Command War Diaries* (1990 ed)

27 April, 1944

On the night of 27/28 April, 1944, Bomber Command sent 144 aircraft to attack the railway yards at the Belgian town of Montzen. The raid encountered strong nightfighter opposition and fifteen bombers (10.4 per cent) failed to return. No.6 (RCAF)Group provided fifty-five Halifaxes and lost ten of them (18.2 per cent). One of those was a

No.431 Squdron Halifax MkIII (LK842/SE-N) based at Croft and crewed by pilot Lieutenant JM Earman (USA); Flying Officer WG Dudley (navigator); Flying Officer HW Pond (bomb aimer); Flying Officer DW King (wireless operator/air gunner); Sergeant B Perry (mid upper gunner); Sergeant J. Cooke(rear gunner); and Sergeant J Graham (flight engineer). Earman's aircraft was on its approach to the target when it was intercepted by a night-fighter. One burst of fire caught the bomber's port inner engine, setting ablaze with flames that rapily enveloped the entire wing. Sgt Perry had clipped on his parachute and was moving forward to his escape exit when the Halifax exploded and catapulted him into the night. When he came to, he was upside down and plummeting earthwards in a free fall. The ground was some 2,000ft below him when he pulled the rip cord. Luckily, his parachute deployed and Perry survived to tell the tale. Sadly, none of his crewmates did.

16/17 June, 1944

On the night of 16/17 June, 1944, Bomber Command despatched No.321 aircraft to attack the synthetic oil plant at Sterkrade/Holten. The target was obscured by cloud and thus bombing was scattered and largely ineffective. The same could not be said of the efforts of the defenders:

No.431 Squadron, Croft, January 1944. Pilot Officer 'George' Johnson (standing centre) and Pilot Officer Dick Garrity (seated next to Johnson) at debriefing following a sortie to Berlin. (DND/PL 26434)

nightfighters accounted for some twenty-one bombers and a further ten fell to flak (a loss rate of 9.7 per cent). No.77 Squadron, Full Sutton, lost 30.4 per cent of the twenty-three Halifaxes they contributed.

The Croft-based squadrons each lost four Halifaxes. One of them was No.431 Squadron's LK837/*SE-H*, piloted by Pilot Officer EO 'George' Johnson, who was on his twenty-second trip. He ordered his crew to bale out when his aircraft caught fire after being struck by flak, but only navigator Dick Garrity managed to get out before the bomber exploded. He was the sole survivor.

SE-H was over Holland when the order was given. Garrity landed safely and subsequently made contact with the Dutch Resistance; eighty-two days later he was back in England. His navigator colleague Flying Officer Roy Carter was less fortunate. Forced to bale out of NA515/*SE-B* (Flying Officer G Blatchford-pilot), Carter was also aided by the Dutch Resistance − but he was subsequently captured by the Germans and shot.

No.431 Squadron, Croft (date unknown). 'Waiting to go was the worst part of it'. Serious faces and one forced smile characterize these aircrew members as they await transport to their Halifaxes. One cannot help wondering how many of them survived the conflict. Left to right: Sergeant J Cooke, Sergeant W Berry, Sergeant C Bull, Warrant Officer WJ MacStocker, Flying Officer W Dudley, Flying Officer K Schubert, Flying Officer H Pond, Flying Officer D King, and Warrant Officer AM Casey. (DND/PL29208)

25 June, 1944. A No.431 Squadron Halifax over the V-1 (flying bomb) site at Gorenflos, near Abbeville. (DND/PL30780)

Croft, 23 October, 1944. No.431 and No.434 Squadron crews are briefed prior to raiding Essen. The station CO, Group Captain RS Turnbull, No.434 Squadron CO Wing Commander AL Blackburn are seated in the aisle. (DND/PL33941)

Croft aerodrome, 11.35am 22 March, 1945. Lancaster KB832/WL-F of No.434 (Bluenose) Squadron disappears in a cloud of fire and smoke. Half an hour earlier, the aircraft had crashed and burst into flames while attempting to take off to attack the railway marshalling yards at Hildesheim. Thankfully, the pilot (Flying Officer Horace Payne) and his crew were able to get well away before the bomb load, which included a 4,000lb 'cookie', detonated. (DND/PL44939)

'They were very very happy lads. Bits of lads − 21...22 − but flying fettled them...They had such a perilous time, going over there and seeing their mates not come back...That was the trouble...It was heartbreaking when they were coming in, shot up or in a bad way. One came in and crash-landed on a farm just across the aerodrome. They fought like mad to get the pilot out but...' [Alice Metcalfe, farmer's wife, Dalton-on-Tees 1939-45]

The flypast by the Lancaster of the Battle of Britain Memorial Flight brought the Dalton-on-Tees ceremony to an emotional close. (Peter Simpson)

Dalton-on-Tees memorial, prior to the unveiling, with the Guard of Honour provided by the RAF Regiment, Catterick. (Peter Simpson)

DARLINGTON

At 8.05pm on the evening of 13 January, 1945, Lancaster KB793/*NA-E* of No.428 (Ghost) Squadron, RCAF, crashed at Lingfield Farm, on the east side of Darlington.

The aircraft had left its base at nearby Middleton-St-George at 5.00pm on a cross-country training flight. Its crew was: Pilot Officer Bill McMullen (pilot); Flying Officer Bill Sage (navigator); Flight Sergeant Ted Dykes (rear gunner); Flight Sergeant John Feeley (mid-upper gunner); Flight Sergeant Steve Ratsoy (wireless operator); Flight Sergeant H Sims (bomb aimer) and Sergeant 'Lew' Lewellin (flight engineer).

Sims and Lewellin were 'spares' for the trip, the usual bomb aimer and engineer having been temporarily grounded due to illness. The others had crewed up with McMullen at No.82 Operational Training Unit (Ossington) in August 1944, following a bale out over France.

Bill Sage recalls that:

'On 16 August, 1944, we were sent on a leaflet-dropping raid.

Bill McMullen and his crew, No.428 (Ghost) Squadron, RCAF, Middleton-St-George, 25 December, 1944. Back (L-R): Pilot Officer Bill McMullen (pilot); Flying Officer Bill Sage (navigator); Flying Officer Jimmy Roth (bomb aimer); Flight Sergeant Steve Ratsoy (wireless operator). Front (L-R): an unknown (flight engineer); Flight Sergeant John Feeley (mid-upper gunner); Flight Sergeant Ted Dykes (rear gunner). Jimmy Roth and the unknown flight engineer, both of whom had been temporarily grounded, were not on the trip of 13 January, 1945. (Bill Sage)

We were in a Wellington and near Chartres we had a fire in one of the engines. We turned for home, still on fire and losing 1,000ft a minute. We started baling out at 5,000ft. All landed safely, but our pilot broke a leg. When we returned to base we were eventually crewed up with Bill McMullen.'

Thus, by a strange twist of fate, it was fire that brought McMullen and his crew together; and it would be fire that would force their final separation five months later.

McMullen and his new crew subsequently completed training on four-engined bombers (Halifax and Lancaster) before joining an operational squadron. They were posted to No.428 Bomber Squadron, RCAF at Middleton-St-George on Christmas Eve 1944, but by mid-January they were still waiting to go on operations for the first time: the cross-country flight was a navigation exercise '...to keep Bill Sage sharp...'

At 8.35pm on 13 January the Lancaster was flying eastwards over North Yorkshire at 10,000ft; its uneventful practice flight was drawing to a close and touch-down was expected within ten minutes. In preparation for landing, Bill McMullen indicated his intention to commence losing altitude and Lewellin eased the throttles but left the RPMs at 1950 to maintain an airspeed of 200mph on the descent.

There was nothing to suggest then that anything was amiss and Lewellin recorded in his log: '...all temperatures and pressures normal. All four engines running evenly...'

Five minutes later, when the bomber was well into its descent, Steve Ratsoy reported heavy showers of sparks streaming from the exhaust stacks of the port outer engine. McMullen levelled out in cloud at about 2,000ft and, believing that they were carbon sparks normally associated with low RPM, instructed his engineer to open the throttles and increase the revs to 2,400. The sparks persisted − and Ratsoy noticed that the exhaust cover was beginning to glow red.

Although all engine gauges were reading normal at that time, a piston was in the process of disintegrating. However, an additional complication − also unknown to the crew − was that the feathering boss had fractured (metal fatigue was later suspected) and the line that fed the hydraulically-operated feathering mechanism had burned away.

When, seconds later, Lewellin pressed the feathering button to close down the affected engine, oil was forced through the fractured pipe and on to the red-hot surfaces: a sheet of flame erupted from the exhaust and within seconds the cowling had started to burn away. In the light of the ensuing blaze Ratsoy could see the whole top of the engine. But it was still driving: the attempt to feather had failed.

Subsequent efforts to feather merely fed the flames, while attempts to douse the fire were to no effect because the intensity of the heat had fused the light alloy spray tubes of the Graviner fire extinguisher system.

As the Lancaster approached Darlington the port wing was well alight and, possibly because of the effects of fire on the control surfaces of the port main-plane and the drag caused by the unfeathered port outer engine, the aircraft had begun to fly in broad circles. It was then that McMullen ordered his crew — except the engineer — to prepare to bale out while he and Lewellin opened the engines to full power in an effort to gain height.

Group Captain Turnbull, RCAF Commander of Middleton-St-George, was standing outside of the Officers' Mess at the aerodrome when he saw an orange glow light up the clouds to the west. As he watched, the glow curved towards the aerodrome and then swung away again. He watched for some three minutes before the plane broke cloud at 1,500ft — by which time the orange glow had changed to the white of burning metal.

Five of the crew exited in cloud at 2,000ft: Sims, Sage and Ratsoy went out through the nose hatch in that order, while John Feeley left via the main door and Ted Dykes direct from his rear turret. The pilot ordered Lewellin out soon afterwards. Before he jumped, the engineer stood by the escape hatch for a moment to see if he was being followed — but Bill McMullen was still at the controls.

The pilot retained control of his machine until it was some 600ft above the ground, but by then it was well ablaze on the port side. Those who had baled out had not reached the ground before the port wing of the stricken Lancaster dipped earthwards. The bomber passed low over the housetops of Darlington's Eastborne district and then cartwheeled into the fields of Lingfield Farm, on the eastern edge of Darlington at what is now the junction of Kellaw Road and Allington Way.

McMullen died instantly when he and the seat in which he was still strapped were catapulted through the windscreen and were later recovered 120 yards from the first point of impact: the flying boots he had been wearing were found in the aircraft — still in the rudder pedals.

Five days later, with his crew in attendance, Bill McMullen was buried with full military honours at the RCAF cemetery, Stonefall, Harrogate, where he still lies.

Bill McMullen as a Flight Sergeant c. August 1943. (via A. Macdonald)

There is also a possibility that McMullen could have baled out, had he so wished, but it is generally believed that he elected to stay with his aircraft in order to steer it away from the town. John Feeley also maintains that his pilot did not want to risk the circling aircraft flying through the descending parachutes, although the mid-upper gunner still clearly remembers that when he was drifting earthwards he saw the Lancaster coming towards him with 'all four propellers whirling'.

The RCAF never publicly acknowledged the Canadian's bravery but citizens of Darlington have done so on at least four occasions. Shortly after the cessation of hostilities, the town honoured his heroism by dedicating two children's cots to his memory at the town's Memorial Hospital. On 19 September, 1945, his sister Mae, who was then serving in England as a member of the Canadian Red Cross, unveiled the commemorative plaque in the children's ward. In 1946 the town's Lingfield Lane was re-named McMullen Road, and a year later (in June 1947) an inscribed silver bowl was presented to McMullen's widow in Canada on behalf of a group of Darlington businessmen, known locally as The Twenty Club.

More recently, following the 40th anniversary of VE-Day, Darlington councillors erected a commemorative plaque close to the site of the crash. It was unveiled by the (then) Mayor, Councillor Joe Anderson, on 6 May, 1986. It stands at the junction of McMullen Road and Allington Way.

Inscription:

The following inscription appears alongside the RCAF crest on a stainless steel plaque.

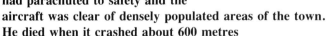

Erected in memory of Pilot Officer William S. McMullen of No.428 Squadron Royal Canadian Air Force who on 13th January 1945, stayed at the controls of his burning Lancaster bomber KB 793 until six members of his crew had parachuted to safety and the aircraft was clear of densely populated areas of the town. He died when it crashed about 600 metres south east of this plaque at Lingfield Farm and was buried at Harrogate with others of the RCAF. McMullen Road was named in tribute to his courage.

No.425 (Alouette) Squadron, No.426 (Thunderbird) Squadron and No.1664 (Caribou) Heavy Conversion Unit, RCAF

DISHFORTH

Dishforth aerodrome is located alongside the A1 trunk road, to the south of the North Yorkshire village from which it takes its name. Opened as a grass airfield in September 1936 and modified in the summer of 1943 to accommodate four-engined heavy bombers, Dishforth was home to three Royal Air Force squadrons − Nos.10, 51 and 78 − before being handed over to the Canadians when No.6 (RCAF) Group was created in January 1943.

No.425 (Alouette) Squadron, RCAF, was the fifth Canadian squadron − and the first French-Canadian unit − to be formed overseas. It was established at Dishforth on 25 June, 1942, as part of No.4 Group Bomber Command but was transferred to No.6 (RCAF) Group in the first month of the new year. It operated Wellington Mk.IIIs from August 1942 until the following April, when it re-equipped with the Mk X version. The Squadron was posted to North Africa on 16 May, 1943, returning to Dishforth six months later (6 November). Its stay there was destined to be a short one for on 10 December, 1943, No.425 (Alouette) Squadron severed its ties with Dishforth and moved to Tholthorpe preparatory to converting to Halifax Mk.IIIs.

No.425 (Alouette) Squadron carried out its first operation − and sustained its first casualties − on the night of 5/6 October, 1942, when eight of its Wellingtons formed part of a force of 257 aircraft launched against Aachen. Ten aircraft (3.9 percent) failed to return from that operation. The Alouettes lost one Wellington (X3843/*KW-G*), which plunged to earth near Debden (Essex) while en route to the target. The five-man crew − Sergeant MF O'Driscoll, Sergeant JB Sandiford, Sergeant T Howells, Sergeant JM Armstrong and Flight Sergeant AC Challis − perished in the crash.

During the period of its service with Nos.4 and 6 Groups, No.425 (Alouette) Squadron launched 225 raids (2,927 sorties) at a cost of thirty-nine (1.3 percent) aircraft lost.[1] During the time spent at Dishforth the Squadron carried out sixty-three raids and lost eleven Wellington bombers − most of which were carrying a crew of six.

No.426 (Thunderbird) Squadron was formed at Dishforth on 15 October, 1942, as the seventh Canadian bomber squadron overseas, and was initially equipped with Wellington Mk IIIs, which were exchanged for the Mk.X version during the following March.

The Thunderbirds went to war for the first time on 14 January, 1943, when they launched their first of eight attacks in five weeks against the important U-Boat base at Lorient, in the Bay of Biscay. In the ensuing months, the emphasis shifted to heavily defended targets in Germany, principally the munitions' centres of the Ruhr − including Cologne, Duisburg, Essen, and Bochum − as well as German ports and industrial centres of the Rhineland. The Squadron was destined to lose eleven Wellingtons over the Ruhr, including that of its first Commanding Officer, Wing Commander SS Blanchard, who failed to return from a raid on Cologne in February 1943. Operations with Wellingtons continued until June 1943, when the Squadron commenced conversion to Lancasters. This coincided with the move to Linton-on-Ouse, where the Squadron was destined to stay until the end of the European campaign.

During the time that it operated from Dishforth, No.426 Squadron carried out 447 sorties on thirty-six bombing and nineteen minelaying operations. These at a cost of twenty aircraft lost (including eleven over the Ruhr) with personnel casualties of ninety-four killed or presumed dead and ten prisoners or 'safe'[2]

The war service of No.426 (Thunderbird) Squadron spanned January 1943 to April 1945, during which time the Squadron participated in 241 raids, including nineteen mining operations (3,207 sorties in total) at a cost of sixty-eight aircraft lost over enemy territory, with a further seven (Lancasters) crashed in England.[3] In the course of operations members of the Squadron won 176 decorations and honours − at a price: 425 personnel killed, presumed dead or missing, and 133 prisoners of war or 'safe'; non-operational losses totalled six personnel killed.

The Thunderbirds moved to Linton-on-Ouse on 18 June, 1943; six months later the Alouettes transferred to Tholthorpe. With the exit of No.425 Squadron, Dishforth converted to the role of training station with arrival of No.1664 (Caribou) Heavy Conversion Unit from Croft on 7 December. This unit was destined to stay at Dishforth until 6 April, 1945, when it disbanded.

The task of No.1664 HCU was to train up replacement crews for No.6 Group. However, a combination of inexperienced trainees and (sometimes) 'clapped out' aircraft no longer deemed fit for operational duties meant that crashes were not uncommon. The first fatal accident following the unit's arrival occurred at 11.38pm 23 December, 1943, when a Halifax Mk V (EB191) broke up over Harrogate and crashed in the town's Kent Road, killing Flight Sergeant ML John (pilot), Sergeant CR Choma (air gunner), and Sergeant J Quinn (flight engineer).

Accidents were a regular feature of *all* training units and No.1664 HCU was no exception. However, October 1944, proved to be a particularly bad month in which six Halifaxes were lost and 24 crew killed in training accidents.

Hugh Naylor, now Clerk to Dishforth Parish Council, grew up alongside the aerodrome at Skipton on Swale and in adulthood he farmed there. When he retired, he settled in Dishforth. On the outskirts of the village there is a sizeable war cemetery of seventy-eight graves (fifty-seven being those of Canadians) of airmen who lost their lives whilst operating from the nearby aerodrome.

However, it is rather off the beaten track and not easily found. Hugh Naylor felt that there was a need for a more 'public' memorial. As he was to subsequently point out:

'It is nearly fifty years since these young men...came and helped to defend the freedom of this country and yet to the casual visitor to this village there is no tangible record of the part played by them, unless they know of the war graves in the cemetery...'

In July 1990, with the aid of fellow villagers Jim Lister and Arlie Wilkinson, he embarked upon a local fund-raising programme. Additional financial help was provided by squadron organisations in Canada, largely through the efforts of Bill Michener, the English representative of No.426 Squadron veterans in this country (who would also later be instrumental in getting C Dale of Thirsk to erect the cairn).

The memorial was unveiled on 29th July, 1991, by appointed ex-Squadron members during a dedication ceremony led by Reverend David Baker, Vicar of Dishforth and Chaplain to No.9 Regiment Army Air Corps. At the same ceremony all members of No.425 and No.426 Squadrons were made Honorary Freemen of the parish.

RCAF Memorial, Dishforth

The memorial, which consists of a block of white rough-hewn stone surmounted by a sundial, stands alongside the village church, inside of which there hangs a framed Roll of Honour bearing seventy-eight names of men of the Air Forces of three nations : Royal Air Force (twenty); Royal Canadian Air Force (fifty-seven); and Royal Australian Air Force (one).

One face of the stone carries a simple brass plate which bears the inscription shown below:

1. HALPENNY (1982) states figures which differ markedly from those given in *Bomber Command War Diaries*. He quotes 3,665 sorties in 287 operations with fifty-five aircraft failing to return; a further eleven are listed as being lost in non-operational incidents. Casualties listed included operational losses of 338 aircrew, of whom 190 are listed as killed or missing, and non-operational losses of sixty-four killed. CASSELS (1991) agrees with HALPENNY'S losses of aircraft but gives the number of sorties as 3,694.

2. Figures taken from *A History of 426 (Thunderbird) Squadron*

3. *A History of 426 (Thunderbird) Squadron* lists 3,233 sorties arising from 242 raids *and* nineteen mining operations and seven sea searches. Aircraft losses are shown as seventy due to operations with a further eighteen crashed in England.

4/5 April, 1943

On the night of 4/5 April, 1943, Bomber Command despatched 577 aircraft to Kiel. Twelve (2.1 percent) failed to return, including a Wellington piloted by Flying Officer DL Kennedy. This aircraft suffered such severe damage when it was hit by flak on the run up to the target that Kennedy jettisoned his bombs and turned for home. En route to the coast, the bomber was intercepted by a Ju88 nightfighter. The Wellington survived the encounter but critical damage to its hydraulics system caused the undercarriage to drop and the bomb-doors to fall open. With the additional drag causing a drain on fuel supplies, the return trip across the North Sea would certainly have been precarious and it cannot have been without its tensions. They almost made it, but five minutes from the English coast the tanks ran dry and Kennedy was forced to ditch his aircraft on the sea.

The Wellington broke up on impact. Pilot Officer D Laskey (bomb aimer) and Sergeant L Anderson (wireless operator) survived the crash and were able to right the capsized dinghy and clamber aboard to await rescue by a destroyer some hours later. The other members of the crew fared less well: Flying Officer Kennedy's body was subsequently washed ashore but Pilot Officer DM Walley (navigator) and Sergeant CN Beaton (rear gunner) were never seen again.

21 March, 1944

The principal purpose of the Heavy Conversion Units was to train up replacement crews destined to fly four-engine heavy bombers, but preparations for operational flying were also integrated into the programme at every opportunity. Sometimes such preparations might include cross-country trips carried out at night to give crews opportunities to practise evading nightfighters and searchlights; sometimes trainee crews might be used in feint attacks against lightly defended targets, thus fulfilling a decoy role for a Main Force raid with the intention of creating confusion among defenders; or sometimes HCU crews were used for 'Nickel' raids, which involved the dropping of propaganda leaflets over a designated town or city in Occupied Europe.

The accident rate in HCU units tended to be quite high: the

Dishforth cemetery contains seventy-eight graves of Allied airmen (fifty-seven of them Canadians) who were killed during the Second World War

combination of inexperienced crews and (sometimes) 'war weary' aircraft no longer deemed fit for operational flying could prove to be a recipe for disaster. One such accident occurred one night in the early Spring of 1944, but the 'inexperienced' pilot proved himself equal to the task.

Halifax II (LK930) had already seen operational service with No.428 (Ghost) Squadron and No.429 (Bison) Squadron before it was re-assigned to No.1664 HCU, Dishforth. On 21 March, 1944, it was detailed to take part in a 'Nickel' raid over France. The crew for the operation was: R Collver (pilot); R Pilkington (navigator); ? Peel (bomb-aimer); R Pym, RAF (flight-engineer); W Loucks (wireless operator); W Andrews (mid-upper gunner); and C Starnes (rear gunner).

As LK930 was approaching the French coast, the order for the raid was rescinded and the aircraft was re-called. On the return journey the starboard outer engine suffered a severe malfunction, which resulted in an over-speeding propeller and extreme vibration — the latter being so bad that it caused the starboard inner engine to fail. Collver managed to reach England but as the Halifax crossed Derbyshire the vibrations worsened and the altimeter started to unwind. The pilot ordered the crew to bale out, but only Pilkington, Peel and Loucks managed to do so before the bomber crash-landed on uneven ground between the villages of Palterton and Scarcliffe, some six miles east of Chesterfield. Collver was thrown clear when the skidding Halifax collided with a small hill and burst into flames. Starnes, Pym and Andrews were trapped inside but were eventually dragged from the burning wreck by two brothers who lived nearby and who had been awakened by the crash.

The courage of George and Albert Calow was subsequently given official acknowledgement when they were each awarded the British Empire Medal. However, their worthy efforts were ultimately to no avail — for the three men for whom they had risked their own lives later died from their injuries.

Dishforth memorial march past 1 July, 1991. (Northern Echo)

CONCRETE CENOTAPH

Sightless now, once watchful eyes,
Blank or shuttered to stormy skies;
Through shattered glass and twisted frames
The keening winds proclaim the names
of those — or so they said,
Were members of the living dead.
For many, true, their time short leased,
Death prevailed and living ceased.

Some still come, we that remain,
To pause and live those times again.
To linger and to wonder why,
We should live whilst others died.
A lot of luck, no doubt of that,
Your number taken from a hat?
A raffle for the Devil's hod-
Or was it by the grace of God?

Rex Polendine

147

No.405 (Vancouver) Squadron, No.408 (Goose) Squadron, No.419 (Moose) Squadron, No.427 (Lion) Squadron and No.429 (Bison) Squadron, RCAF

LEEMING

The RCAF memorial of Yorkshire sandstone stands on the roadside outside the Church of St John the Baptist, Leeming village. It was unveiled on 19 June, 1993, during a service of dedication and remembrance which was led by the Right Reverend Malcolm Menim, Bishop of Knaresborough, in the presence of some 100 Canadian veterans, a number of serving personnel who had been flown over from Canada for the occasion, and many members of the general public. Special guests included Group Captain Dudley Burnside DSO DFC★ RAF (Ret'd), the first Commanding Officer of No.427 (Lion) Squadron; Lieutenant-General A Chester Hull CMM DFC CD(Ret'd) who commanded No.428 (Ghost) Squadron from August 1944 to January 1945; Group Captain PW Roser, Officer Commanding RAF Leeming; and representatives of Leeming parish council led by Mr F Herbert and Mr A Baker, both of whom had been actively involved in the Leeming Memorial Committee.

The memorial was unveiled by representatives of three of the Canadian squadrons based there during the war: Group Captain D Burnside DSO

The RCAF Memorial in Leeming village.

OBE DFC *(ex-427); S Puskas DFC (ex-429); and Mr D Petteys (ex-408). The proceedings were brought to a close with a flypast provided by a Spitfire of the Battle of the Britain Memorial Flight.

The column of Yorkshire sandstone bears a plaque set above carvings of a maple leaf and a Yorkshire Rose. The following inscription appears on the plaque below the crests of the RCAF and the RAF.

This memorial is dedicated to those
men and women who served at RAF Leeming
during World War II, including those from
Royal Canadian Air Force Squadrons,
whose members came from all parts of
the Commonwealth from 1942 to 1945:

405 Vancouver 408 Goose 419 Moose
427 Lion 429 Bison

also to the many civilians who supported
them during their term of duty in North
Yorkshire. We remember too the RAF
Squadrons who preceded the Canadians
from 1940 to 1942:

7 – 10 – 35 – 77 – 102 – 219

TO THOSE WHO PAID THE SUPREME SACRIFICE
WE WILL REMEMBER THEM

Dedicated June 19, 1993

Leeming aerodrome opened in June 1940 as part of No.4 Group Bomber Command. Nos.7, 35, and 102 Squadrons had very short postings there while in transit, and the Catterick-based No.219 Squadron had a detachment of Blenheims there during the first year of the war, but No.10 Squadron (July 1940 – August 1942) and No.77 Squadron (September 1941 – May 1942) spent substantial time there before August 1942, when Canadian units started to move in preparatory to the airfield's transfer to No.6 (RCAF) Group on 1 January, 1943.

Although the Leeming Memorial commemorates five RCAF Squadrons (and acknowledges the RAF units) that served there during the Second World War, only three of those spent any length of time at

D Petteys (left), S Puskas (centre) and Group Captain Burnside (right) unveil the Leeming Memorial.

Spitfire flypast at the Leeming Memorial.

Group Captain Dudley Burnside DSO DFC★ RAF (Ret'd), one-time CO of No.427 (Lion) Squadron, RCAF, seen here wearing the uniform of Honorary Lieutenant-Colonel of the Royal Canadian Air Force.

19 June, 1993. Second World War veterans of No.429 (Bison) Squadron, RCAF, join with serving personnel at the Leeming memorial.

the station. No.405 (Vancouver) Squadron was at the North Yorkshire base for only four weeks (in March/April 1943) before transferring to Gransden Lodge (Huntingdon) and the Pathfinder Force. No.419 (Moose) Squadron's stay was even shorter: less than one week (in August 1942) before the unit moved in quick succession to Topcliffe, Croft and Middleton-St-George, where the Moosemen finally settled for the war's duration. Although it does not feature on the memorial plaque, No.424 (Tiger) Squadron also spent a short time at Leeming during April/May 1943 before moving first to Dalton and then to Skipton-on-Swale. Thus, for the period of its service with No.6 (RCAF) Group, Leeming is more closely associated with No.408 (Goose), No.427 (Lion) and No.429 (Bison) Squadrons.

*   *   *

No.408 (Goose) Squadron was formed at Lindholme (as part of No.5 Group) on 15 June, 1941, and was equipped with Hampden bombers. A month later they moved to Syerston (Notts), where they stayed for five months before moving on to Balderton (Notts). The Squadron re-located to Leeming on 14 September, 1942, and converted to the Halifax Mk V, a type they operated for some three months before re-equipping with the Halifax Mk II. The move to Linton-on-Ouse on 27 August, 1943, saw the beginning of a more settled period and No.408 did not change location again until their move to Canada in mid-June 1945.

During the period 1941-1945 the Squadron carried out 457 raids and 4453 sorties. These operations resulted in the loss of 129 (2.9 percent) aircraft, with a further ten (Lancasters) being destroyed in crashes. Although precise losses of crews are not known, these aircraft losses represent some 980 personnel, most of whom would have been killed or 'missing, presumed killed' − for such was the nature of Bomber Command's war.[1]

*   *   *

No.427 (Lion) Squadron RCAF was formed at Croft as part of No.4 Group on 7 November, 1942, and operated the Wellington MkIII until February 1943, when the type was replaced by the Mk X version. On 5 May, 1943, the Squadron moved to Leeming and stayed for the duration of the European war. They changed aircraft three times while at Leeming: to the Halifax Mk V, in May 1943; to the Halifax Mk III (January 1944); and the Lancaster Mk I and Mk III (March 1945).

Prior to January 1943, No.427 (Lion) Squadron flew only one (mine-laying) operation. During its operational career with No.6 (RCAF) Group it flew a total of 3,309 sorties in 217 operations, and lost sixty-nine (2.1 percent) aircraft.[2]

*   *   *

No.429 (Bison) Squadron was formed at Eastmoor as part of No.4 Group on 7 November, 1942 and was equipped with the Wellington Mk III until the following January, when the Mk X version was introduced. The Squadron transferred to No.6 (RCAF) Group on 1 April, 1943. Their move to Leeming, in August 1943, coincided with conversion to the Halifax Mk II, a type that they operated for three months before being assigned the Halifax Mk V. In March 1944 the Halifax Mk III was introduced to the Squadron and was not replaced until twelve months later, when they re-equipped with the Lancaster Mk I and Mk III.

During the Second World War No.429 (Bison) Squadron flew 3175 sorties in 267 operations and lost 78 aircraft (2.5 percent).[3]

1. CASSELS (1991) claims that No.408 Squadron lost 146 aircraft on 4,610 sorties with a further twelve being lost in non-operational incidents. HALPENNY (1982) confirms this number and gives the casualties as 877 killed, missing or POW as a result of operations, with a further thirty-two killed and 7 injured due to non-operational incidents. Awards to crews were: one MBE; 161 DFCs; six Bars to DFC; thirty-two DFMs; and ten Mentions in Despatches.

2. HALPENNY (1982) claims that No.427 Squadron carried out 3,328 sorties, at a cost of ninety aircraft and 522 crew, of whom thirty-five were killed and 456 missing. Awards to crews amounted to four DSOs; 147 DFCs; six bars to DFC; one AFC; two CGMs; sixteen DFMs; and eight Mentions in Despatches. CASSELS (1991) agrees the number of sorties and the number of aircraft lost on operations as stated by HALPENNY, but he raises the number of aircraft lost to ninety-six, by adding six aircraft lost during non-operational duties.

3. HALPENNY (1982) gives the figures for No.429 Squadron as 3,221 sorties carried out and seventy-one aircraft lost. Crew losses are given as 451, made up of eighty-two killed, 322 missing, twenty-three prisoners of war and twenty-four safe. Awards are listed as: forty-five DFCs; 2 Bars to DFC; one AFC; one CGM; and seven DFMs. CASSELS (1991) states operational losses in aircraft as being seventy-one but he adds eleven for losses on non-operational duties, thus raising the total figure to eighty-two.

12/13 March, 1943

On the night of 12/13 March, 1943, 457 bombers were despatched to attack the Krupp armament complex at Essen. No.427 (Lion) Squadron, then based at Croft, put up eleven Wellingtons, one of which (BK164/*ZL-E*) was flown by the Squadron's English CO, Wing Commander Burnside DFC. Dudley Burnside clearly led by example and had made a point of ensuring that he flew on all of the toughest operations. Essen had always been difficult − and the night of 12/13 March, 1944, was to provide its own test for him and his crew.

On its approach to the target, *ZL-E* was caught in a barrage of flak: navigator Warrant Officer Rod Heather was killed instantly and wireless operator Flight Sergeant Geoffrey Keene DFM (a veteran of thirty-eight operational flights had part of his right foot severed and both legs badly lacerated when splintered steel tore through the aircraft. Shrapnel also damaged wireless equipment and aileron controls, as well as puncturing the windscreen de-icing tank. The effect of the latter was to fill the bomb-aimer's compartment with choking fumes and drench Pilot Officer RJ Hayhurst with glycol. Shortly afterwards, the oxygen system failed and Burnside had to reduce altitude to 10,000ft − but he pressed on, Hayhurst staying at his post to direct his captain over the target before successfully unloading his bombs.

Over Essen, the Wellington was coned by searchlights for some minutes before Burnside finally managed to make good his escape and turn westwards. Without Heather to guide them to safety, Flight Sergeant Keene helped his pilot with the navigation of the aircraft 'and twice dragged himself to the navigator's compartment to obtain essential information.' This in spite of his cruel injuries and the intense pain that he must surely have felt. That task completed, he then toiled for two hours to repair his damaged wireless. Over the Dutch coast the crew had a further brush with danger when they were intercepted by two nightfighters. However, those were fought off by gunner Pilot Officer DB Ross, who also gave Burnside the instructions that ultimately led to successful evasion.

Twenty-eight aircraft (5.0 percent) failed to return from the Essen raid of 12/13 March, 1943: Wellington BK164/*ZL-E* was among the lucky ones, although Burnside was unable to reach Croft and had to set down at Stradishall (Suffolk).

> 'As was only fitting, the very fine display of courage and determination shown by all members of the crew was subsequently recognised by awards. Burnside received a Bar to his DFC, Hayhurst and Ross the DFC, and Keene, who already had the DFM, the Conspicuous Gallantry Medal.' (*RCAF Overseas* 1944)

Wing Commander Dudley Burnside and his crew, No.427 (Lion) Squadron, RCAF, Croft, early 1943. **L to R:** *Flight Sergeant Ross (air gunner); Flying Officer Hayhurst (bomb-aimer); Wing Commander Burnside (pilot); Flight Sergeant Keene (wireless operator); Warrant Officer Heather (navigator)* (Group Captain Dudley Burnside)

Burnside, backed by 'Bomber' Harris, had recommended Keene for the Victoria Cross, but for some reason this was turned down by 'higher authorities'. Keene's award of the CGM was the first to be granted to a member of the RCAF.

March-September 1943

Bomber crews had to complete a 'tour' of thirty operations over enemy-held territory before being rested for six months from active duties. One crew that participated in the required number of flights was that of Pilot Officer George Vandekerckhove, No.427 (Lion) Squadron RCAF, a squadron which had been formed at Croft on 7 November, 1942, and which remained there until 5 May, 1943, when it moved a little further south to Leeming.

Some of the dangers faced by operational bomber crews during the

Vandekerckhove's crew and their Wellington Mk III (Z1572/ZL-Q) after their return from Essen, 6 March, 1943. (W Williamson)

Second World War are amply illustrated by just four of the trips made by this crew during their time at both operational stations.

5/6 March, 1943. **(ESSEN: 442 bombers detailed; 14 lost).**

During the raid, Vandekerckhove's Wellington Mk III bomber (*Z1572/ZL-Q*) was over the target and on its bomb-run when it was seriously damaged by a nightfighter. The attacker's shells severed the oil line to the starboard engine, thus robbing the bearing of lubricant. Shortly afterwards, the bearing seized up and the engine burst into flames close by the propeller. However, this did not stop Vanderkerckhove from pressing home his attack. The Wellington was still in the target area when the fire was finally extinguished – seconds after the propeller flew off and spiralled earthwards. There is the possibility that the nightfighter suffered a similar fate, for rear gunner Sergeant JJ ('Mac') McLean returned fire and the fighter was seen to dive into the target area: McLean claimed it as a 'probable'.

In spite of having only one enginge, Vandekerckhove decided to make for England. The return trip across the North Sea cannot have been without its tense moments, for that particular stretch of water is a hostile environment at any time. They managed it (but not without some loss of altitude en route) and made landfall north of Hull shortly before landing safely at Catfoss – without the aid of hydraulics. George Vandekerckhove was subsequently recommended for an award for his airmanship and in August 1943 he received the DFC for his efforts.

29/30 July, 1943. **(HAMBURG: 77 bombers detailed; 28 lost).**

Based at Leeming and flying a Halifax Mk V, Vanderkerckhove and

Vandekerckhove's Halifax crew 1943. Back row (L-R): *Pilot Officer 'Den' Rothwell (bomb-aimer); Sergeant 'Ted' Bartlett (flight engineer); Pilot Officer 'Van' Vandekerckhove (pilot); Pilot Officer 'Willie' Williamson (navigator).* Middle row (extreme right): *Flight Sergeant 'Johnny' Albert (mid-upper gunner).* Front row (in harness): *Sergeant Alan Young (wireless operator)* on the left; Warrant Officer 'Mac' McLean (rear gunner) on the right.

(W Williamson)

his crew survived being 'coned' by 40-50 searchlights, escaped the accompanying flak barrage, and successfully countered two attacks by nightfighters (Sergeant McLean being credited with one Ju88 'probable' damaged) to return home 'almost unscathed'.

2/3 August, 1943. (**HAMBURG: 740 bombers detailed; 30 lost**).

'Van' and his crew had to rely on Pathfinder flares when they bombed the target in a severe thunderstorm. As they turned west at the start of their homeward journey an aircraft alongside exploded and 'flipped' them over. They plummeted out of control for 15,000ft, the pilot's difficulties being aggravated by the fact that icing affected the carburettors in all engines. When he managed to regain some control at 4,000 ft, two engines were out of action and two were coughing and spluttering. They crossed Northern Germany at the potentially very dangerous height of 4,000ft and were thus highly vulnerable to flak and to nightfighters. However, luck was with them. As they flew out over the sea, the flight engineer got the engines working again and they returned safely to Leeming without further trouble.

Pilot Officer George Vandekerckhove, No.427 (Lion) Squadron, RCAF. (via Mrs A Metcalfe)

31 August/1 September, 1943. **(BERLIN: 622 aircraft detailed; 47 lost).** This was to be their thirtieth trip: on their return they would be rested for six months from active duties. As on all the Berlin raids, the bombers encountered very severe flak and rigorous nightfighter attacks. Forty-seven aircraft failed to return from this operation: Vandekerckhove's was one of them. Although he and his crew participated in thirty operations, only two members were destined to survive the final flight. When their aircraft was shot down in flames over the target only 'Den' Rothwell (bomb-aimer) and 'Willie' Williamson (navigator), managed to bale out before the wounded Halifax struck the earth. Six members of the crew perished: Rothwell and Williamson spent the rest of the war as prisoners-of-war. Fifty years on 'Willie' Williamson describes what happened that night:

"We were flying a spare aircraft (*ZL-T*) on our last trip. The aircraft wouldn't climb beyond 15,000ft so we became a straggler behind our wave. We were in 10/10 cloud when we were hit by cannon-fire from directly below (a Ju88 pilot on a 'drome where I was taken after capture said it was a *schräge musik* attack). The cannon shells set the wing on fire. During a second attack the wing came off and we went into a spin. I sat over the escape hatch in the nose and was able to bale out just before we crashed. I landed in woods in the pitch black rain and heard our aircraft explode in the distance. I evaded for seven days but was captured while crossing into Holland. 'Den', the bomb-aimer, baled out of the back door, where he was throwing out bales of silver foil ('window'). He was captured immediately and we later met up in POW camp. The remaining six members died in the crash. They included a second pilot – Cam Goften – on his first trip. They were buried near Osnabruck and later re-buried at Reichswald War Cemetery, near Kleve."

Just beyond the Station HQ a Canadian maple tree, planted at Leeming in May 1987, reminds passers-by of time spent at the base by No.427 (Lion) Squadron and No.429 (Bison) Squadrons RCAF.

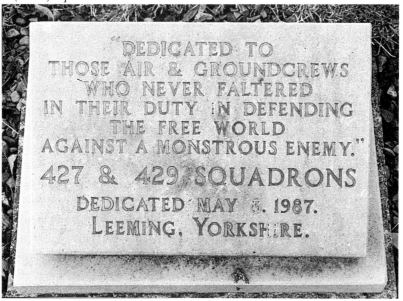

7/8 June, 1944

Halifax bombers from No.4 Group were among the 337 aircraft detailed to attack a number of railway targets in France on the night of 7/8 June, 1944. The raiders were intercepted by nightfighters and it is likely that

IN COMMEMORATION
OF THOSE MEN AND WOMEN OF MANY NATIONS
WHO SERVED AT RAF LEEMING
DURING THE SECOND WORLD WAR

No 10 SQN RAF	JUL 1940 - AUG 1942
No 77 SQN RAF	SEP 1941 - MAY 1942
No 419 (MOOSE) SQN RCAF	AUG 1942 - SEP 1942
No 408 (GOOSE) SQN RCAF	SEP 1942 - AUG 1943
No 405 (VANCOUVER) SQN RCAF	MAR 1943 - APR 1943
No 427 (LION) SQN RCAF	MAY 1943 - MAY 1946
No 429 (BISON) SQN RCAF	AUG 1943 - MAY 1946

UNVEILED BY
AIR VICE-MARSHAL M K ADAMS AFC FRAeS RAF
AIR OFFICER COMMANDING TRAINING UNITS
29 JUNE 1983

A commemorative plaque dedicated to all personnel who served at Leeming during the Second World War was unveiled in June 1983. It stands in front of the Station HQ.

most of the twenty-eight bombers (8.3 percent) lost on that operation succumbed to airborne defenders, but flak also took its toll.

Halifax Mk III (LW128/AL-V), of No.429 (Bison) Squadron, Leeming, was peppered by shrapnel 18,000ft over Dieppe while en-route to its target at Acheres. The pilot, Squadron Leader WB Anderson DFC, was mortally wounded when a shell fragment struck him in the side; he ordered his crew to bale out and then slumped into unconsciousness over the control column as the bomber went into a vertical dive.

Flight Sergeant A Capustan (navigator), Sergeant LS O'Leary (bomb-aimer), and Warrant Officer JD Banning (wireless operator) jumped, but as the Halifax plummeted earthwards Flight Sergeant Gilbert Steere (flight engineer) dragged Anderson from the cockpit, wrestled with the controls and eventually eased the aircraft out of its dive. At that point he was joined by Sergeant John Mangione (mid-upper gunner) and Flight Sergeant Gordon Ritchie (rear gunner), who had been making their way towards the escape exits when they realized that the Halifax was levelling out.

Anderson was their priority and the gunners administered pain-killing morphine to their pilot and rendered what First Aid they were able to while Steere — who was not a pilot — attempted to settle down to the

Three members of No.429 (Bison) Squadron RCAF Leeming who were decorated after flying their Halifax back to England on the night of 7/8 June, 1944, when their pilot had been mortally wounded over Dieppe. (L to R) Sergeant John Mangione DFM; Sergeant Gilbert Steere (RAF) CGM; and Flight Sergeant Gordon Ritchie DFM. (DND/UK12647)

task of getting the Halifax and its occupants back to base as best as he could. The bomb-load was jettisoned near Dieppe and the bomber turned for home.

On the return trip, Steere's difficulties were heightened by the fact that he could not see out of the cockpit: he was wearing a chest pack parachute and thus he was sitting too low in the pilot's bucket seat to be able to see through the windscreen. He had to rely solely upon the artificial horizon instrument in order to gauge the aircraft's attitude in flight: the return trip 'was anything but a smooth flight back'. Nevertheless, they made it.

Once over land, and given Gilbert Steere's (understandable) unwillingness to risk a landing, it was decided that a bale out was the only option. Mangione and Ritchie clipped Anderson's parachute to a static line and after explaining their purpose to the gravely wounded pilot they dropped him out through the escape hatch before they too made their exits; Steere followed soon afterwards. They and their aircraft came to earth half a mile north east of RAF Benson [near Wallingford (Oxfordshire)], Ritchie having the unnerving experience of landing alongside a marked minefield.

Steere, Mangione and Ritchie survived their ordeal, but Anderson did not. His body was recovered and was later buried in Brookwood Cemetery, Woking (Surrey). The bomb aimer and the wireless operator were at liberty for a short time before they were captured and made prisoners of war. The navigator had better luck: he established contact with the French Resistance and returned to England six weeks later.

On 14 June, 1944, in recognition of his achievement, Gilbert Steere was awarded the Conspicuous Gallantry Medal; John Mangione and Gordon Ritchie were awarded the Distinguished Flying Medal.

No.408 (Goose) Squadron and No.426 (Thunderbird) Squadron, RCAF

LINTON-ON-OUSE

The decision to erect a memorial stone at Linton-on-Ouse was taken in 1988, during the RCAF biennial reunion which was held at York. The target date for the dedication was set for May 1990, when the Canadian veterans would once again meet in Yorkshire.

The task of finding a suitable site and of arranging for the memorial to be carved fell to Bill Michener, No.426 Squadron Association's UK representative, who worked in collaboration with a Canadian committee consisting of John May, Howie West and Bill Swetman. It was Bill Michener who ultimately commissioned Thirsk-based mason C. Dale, to carve the memorial to a suggested design sent from Canada, and it was he who also found the site on which the monument stands. He was aided in the latter by strong support from the then Commanding Officer of RAF Linton, Group Captain P. Gooding AFC, and the Parish Council (under the Chairmanship of Derek Jauncey), who donated the land.

Inscription:

From June, 1943, to May, 1945, two squadrons of the ROYAL CANADIAN AIR FORCE, part of the all CANADIAN 6 GROUP, BOMBER COMMAND, operated out of the nearby Air Base, achieving a distinguished record and an honoured place in the annals of the ALLIED AIR OFFENSIVE of WORLD WAR II.
This MEMORIAL CAIRN has been erected that we and generations to come might pause and reflect upon the dedication and sacrifice of those who died in the cause of freedom and human dignity
while serving with
408 (GOOSE) SQUADRON and 426 (THUNDERBIRD) SQUADRON
"At the going down of the sun and in the morning, We will remember them."
IN GRATITUDE
We hallow that memory and the spirit that binds us in commitment to those human rights and values for which we strove; a bond forged in a perilous time of shared sacrifice and struggle, triumph and peace.
ERECTED BY
The Associations of former Members of 408 SQUADRON and 426 SQUADRON
and the people of the village of LINTON-ON-OUSE
Dedicated the 4th day of May, 1990

(via Mrs H Kirby)

IN REMEMBRANCE
1939 - 1945

Linton-on-Ouse aerodrome c.1943 (David E Thompson)

The Linton memorial stands in the main street, in front of the village hall. It consists of a rectangular block of Yorkshire stone bearing carvings of the Canadian Maple Leaf and the Yorkshire Rose and is surmounted by an inscribed bronze plaque which was cast in Canada.

The monument was unveiled on 4 May, 1990, by Agnes Sambrook (No.426 Squadron Association) and Phyllis Cowie (No.408 Squadron Association) during a service of remembrance led by Fr. Harry Schmuck (ex-No.426 Squadron rear gunner) and attended by some 380 Canadians. The Official Party consisted of: Sir Marcus Worsley Bart., Lord Lieutenant of North Yorkshire; John May, President, No.426 Association; Group Captain P. Gooding AFC, Commanding Officer RAF Linton; Derek Jauncey, Chairman, Linton Parish Council; Clifford Black, last wartime commander of No.426 Squadron; and Dr S Franklin, No.408 Squadron Association. Honoured guests were Councillor Dr Stanley Wood, Deputy Mayor of Harrogate; Cannon Jack Armstrong, York Minster; Dr Derek Sayner; and Mr Geoff Wood. Jet Provosts of No.1 Flying Training School, Linton, provided the flypast.

No.408 (Goose) Squadron was formed at Lindholme (as part of No.5 Group) on 15 June, 1941, and was equipped with Hampden bombers. A month later they moved to Syerston (Notts), where they stayed for five months before moving on to Balderton (Notts). The Squadron re-located to Leeming on 14 September, 1942, and converted to the Halifax Mk V, a type they operated for some three months before re-equipping with the Halifax Mk II. The move to Linton-on-Ouse on 27 August, 1943, saw the beginning of a more settled period and No.408 did not change location again until their move to Canada in mid-June 1945.

The Squadron changed aircraft type four times during their stay at Linton. Two months after their arrival they changed to the Lancaster Mk II and operated the aircraft until September 1944, when they accepted the Halifax Mk III and Mk IV. They reverted to the Lancaster in May 1945, when they converted to the Mk X version.

During the period 1941-1945 the Squadron carried out 457 raids and 4453 sorties. These operations resulted in the loss of 129 (2.9 percent) aircraft, with a further ten (Lancasters) being destroyed in crashes. Although precise losses of crews are not known, these aircraft losses represent some 980 personnel, most of whom would have been killed or 'missing presumed killed' − for such was the nature of Bomber Command's war.[1]

∗   ∗   ∗

No.426 (Thunderbird) Squadron was formed at Dishforth on 15 October, 1942, as the seventh Canadian bomber squadron overseas, and was initially equipped with Wellington Mk IIIs, which were exchanged for the Mk X version during the following March.

The Thunderbirds went to war for the first time on 14 January, 1943, when they launched their first of eight attacks in five weeks against the important U-Boat base at Lorient, in the Bay of Biscay. In the ensuing months, the emphasis shifted to heavily defended targets in Germany, principally the munitions' centres of the Ruhr − Duisburg, Essen, and Bochum − (at a cost of 11 Wellingtons) as well as ports and industrial centres of the Rhineland. Operations with Wellingtons continued until June 1943, when the Squadron moved to Linton-on-Ouse for the remaining years of the war.

No.426 Squadron changed aircraft type four times whilst at Linton: the Lancaster Mk II was adopted one month after their arrival at their new home and was retained until the Halifax Mk III was assigned to the unit in April 1944; three months later the Halifax Mk III was replaced by the Mk VII version but in the following December the Halifax Mk III was re-instated.

The war service of No.426 (Thunderbird) Squadron spanned January 1943 to April 1945, during which time the Squadron participated in 241 raids, including nineteen mining operations (3,207 sorties in total) at a cost of sixty-eight aircraft lost over enemy territory, with a further seven (Lancasters) crashed in England.[2] In the course of operations members of the Squadron won 176 decorations and honours − at a price: 425 personnel killed, presumed dead or missing, and 133 prisoners of war or 'safe'; non-operational losses totalled six personnel killed.

1. CASSELS (1991) claims that No.408 Squadron lost 146 aircraft on 4,610 sorties with a further twelve being lost in non-operational incidents. HALPENNY (1982) confirms this number and gives the casualties as 877 killed, missing or POW as a result of operations, with a further thirty-two killed and seven injured due to non-operational incidents. Awards to crews were: one MBE; 161 DFCs; six Bars to DFC; thirty-two DFMs; and ten Mentions in Despatches.
2. *A History of 426 (Thunderbird) Squadron* lists 3,233 sorties arising from 242 raids *and* nineteen mining operations and seven sea searches. Aircraft losses are shown as seventy due to operations with a further eighteen crashed in England.
   The Royal Canadian Air Force at Linton-on-Ouse, 1942-1945 gives No.426 Squadron's loss figures while at that station as follows: 209 raids (including two sea searches); 2770 sorties (including four aircraft on sea searches); sixty-eight aircraft lost (including nine that crashed on return to England.

Nos.419 (Moose) Squadron, No.420 (Snowy Owl) Squadron and No.428 (Ghost) Squadron, RCAF

MIDDLETON-ST-GEORGE
Co. Durham

The construction of the aerodrome at Middleton-St-George (sometimes known as Goosepool, after a nearby farm) commenced in the second half of 1939 and from January 1941 until December 1943 the airfield formed part of No.4 Group Bomber Command. At various times it was home to Nos.76 and 78 Bomber Squadrons before they moved further south to Linton-on-Ouse in September 1942. One month later, No.420 (Snowy Owl) Squadron moved up from Skipton-on-Swale to begin the base's association with the RCAF that was to last until the end of the war. On 1 January, 1943, Goosepool and the Canadian units stationed there were transferred to No.6 (RCAF) Group.

No.420 Squadron had flown Hampden light-bombers following its formation at Waddington, Lincolnshire, as part of No.5 Group in December 1941. In August 1942, the Squadron was transferred to No.4 Group and was re-located to Skipton-on-Swale, the move northwards

The Middleton-St-George Memorial to Nos.419, 420 and 428 Squadrons RCAF.

coinciding with conversion to Wellington Mk IIIs. In the following February these were discarded in favour of the Mk X version. On 16 October, 1942, the Squadron moved to Middleton-St-George and in the following May was posted to the Middle East for a six month tour of duty. On its return (November 1943), 420 stayed at Dalton for one month before moving to Tholthorpe − its home for the remainder of the war − and converting to the Halifax Mk III. During its operational service, No.420 (Snowy Owl) Squadron carried out a total of 3,479 sorties in 314 raids and lost sixty aircraft; during its Yorkshire-based operations the Squadron flew 2,944 sorties in 224 raids and lost forty-one aircraft.[1] Squadron personnel were awarded thirty-eight DFCs, one Bar to the DFC, and nine DFMs.

*   *   *

No.419 (Moose) Squadron was formed at Mildenhall, Suffolk, on 15 December, 1941, as part of No.3 Group, and was equipped with the Wellington Mk IC and the Mk III. The unit moved northwards in August 1942 and, following very short stays at Leeming, Topcliffe and Croft, took up residence at Middleton-St-George 10 October, 1942. However, unlike No.420 Squadron the 'Moosemen' were destined to stay at Middleton until the cessation of hostilities. In November 1942, the Squadron's Wellingtons were exchanged for the Halifax Mk II, which was used until conversion to the Lancaster Mk X in March 1944.

During its war service, No.419 (Moose) Squadron carried out 4,293 sorties in 354 raids at a cost of 129 (3.0 percent) aircraft lost. In addition, fourteen Lancasters were lost in crashes.[2] 232 of the raids (comprising 3,645 sorties) carried out by the 'Moosemen' were launched from Middleton-St-George and accounted for 105 losses of aircraft. No.419 Squadron held the No.6 Group record for the highest number of raids and sorties undertaken, but it also sustained the highest operational losses of personnel among Canadian squadrons: 528 killed and 167 missing (Elmer 1987). In recognition of this effort, 195 decorations were awarded to members of the Squadron, including one Victoria Cross, which was awarded posthumously to Pilot Officer Andrew Mynarski for his efforts to save a crew-mate on the night of 12 June, 1944,

When No.420 (Snowy Owl) Squadron left for North Africa (in May 1943), they were replaced by No.428 (Ghost) Squadron which, with No.419 Squadron, was to stay at Middleton-St-George until 1945. Although No.428 had formed at Dalton (near Thirsk) in November 1942 as part of No.4 Group, its Wellington Mk IIIs did not start operations until after the formation of No.6 (RCAF) Group, in January 1943. The Squadron converted to Wellington Mk Xs in the following

15 June, 1985. Canadian veterans queue to renew their acquaintance with the Lancaster, in this case the Battle of Britain Memorial Flight's City of Lincoln *which provided the flypast during the unveiling ceremony.* (David E Thompson)

April. Two months later it moved to Middleton, where it converted first to the Halifax Mk II and then subsequently to the Lancaster Mk X. During its time in Yorkshire, No.428 (Ghost) Squadron carried out 3,433 sorties in 268 operations and lost sixty-seven aircraft. In addition, ten Lancasters were lost in accidental crashes.[3]

Both Nos.419 and 428 Squadrons flew their last operation of the Second World War on 25 April, 1945, when fifteen aircraft from each squadron bombed gun-emplacements on the East Frisian island of Wangerooge.

*   *   *

In 1982, former Flight-Lieutenant 'Robby' Robson, an ex-428 Squadron wireless operator/air gunner who had served at Middleton, had a chance meeting with a wartime room-mate. The idea of a reunion of ex-members of the three squadrons grew from that encounter and in turn led to the establishment of a Memorial Committee charged with the task of establishing a monument on the site of the old bomber base. The United Kingdom committee, consisting of 'Robby' Robson, Eddie Scott-Jones and Harry Prendergast, worked in close liaison with their counterparts in Canada: Ken Branston, Doug Gray, Roy Clarke and Jim Gunn. The reunion and the unveiling of the memorial took place in the summer of 1985.

When the RAF decommissioned its base at Middleton-St-George in 1964 the aerodrome became Tees-side airport and the Officers' Mess was converted to the St. George's Hotel. The memorial, flanked by two maple saplings, stands in a small garden at the front of the hotel and commemorates the three RCAF squadrons – Nos.419 (Moose), 420 (Snowy Owl), and 428 (Ghost) – who served there during the last three years of the Second World War.

The monument was unveiled on 15 June, 1985, by Father JP Lardie, RC Chaplain RCAF (Ret'd) at Middleton from 1942 to 1945, during a ceremony attended by some four hundred people, including a large number of veterans who were returning to their wartime base for the first time since 1945. Among the special guests present were civic dignitaries from Stockton-on-Tees and from Darlington, as well as Tees-side Airport officials and a representative of the Canadian Air Defence Staff. The special guest was Mrs Donna Mae Barber, daughter of Pilot Officer Bill McMullen who was killed when his Lancaster crashed at Darlington on 13 January, 1945.

The ceremony was brought to an emotional conclusion when, following the sounding of the *Last Post*, the Battle of Britain Memorial Flight Lancaster *City of Lincoln* performed two low fly-pasts in salute. The Lancaster then landed and was visited throughout the day by veterans 'eager to renew an old acquaintance'. Later, a British Aerospace Mosquito paid its own acknowledgement with several high speed low passes before dipping its wings over the Lancaster and disappearing westwards.

1. HALPENNY (1982) gives the figures as sixty-five aircraft failing to return from operations, with a further three lost due to non-operational causes. Losses of personnel attributable to operations amounted to 324 aircrew, of whom 312 were killed or missing; twelve personnel were killed on non-operational duties.

2. ELMER (1987) gives the total number of sorties as 4,326 (including sea searches) and the number of aircraft lost on operations as 154 (including seventeen lost over England on return from ops). A further ten aircraft were lost in training accidents. Stated casualties amounted to 695 (528 killed and 167 missing).

3. HALPENNY (1982) claims that eighty-four aircraft and 463 aircrew failed to return. Of the latter, sixty-three were killed and 377 posted as missing, believed killed. Squadron personnel were awarded two DSOs, seventy-one DFCs, two CGMs, and six DFMs.

12/13 June, 1944

On the night of 12/13 June, 1944, 671 bombers were launched against railway targets in France: it was a raid from which twenty-three aircraft (3.4 percent) would not return. No.6 (RCAF) Group contributed a combined force of some 200 Halifaxes and Lancasters. One of the latter was a Lancaster Mk X (KB726/*VR-A*), of No.419 (Moose) Squadron, Middleton-St-George, which set out to bomb the marshalling yards at Cambrai from a height of 2,000ft.

The crew of KB726/*VR-A* consisted of Art deBreyne (pilot); Bob Brodie (navigator); Jack Friday (bomb aimer); Roy Vigas, RAF (flight engineer); Jim Kelly (wireless operator); Andrew Mynarski (mid upper gunner); and Pat Brophy (rear gunner). Their average age was twenty-one years. For those among them who were given to superstition, the trip may well have had particular significance: it was their thirteenth operation, and they would be over the target in the early hours of 13th June. However, any foreboding to which such a coincidence may have given rise may well have been assuaged just before take-off, when Mynarski found a four-leaf clover in the grass, and gave it to his friend and rear-gunner, Pat Brophy. Minutes later they were en route to France.

Shortly after crossing the French coast, *VR-A* was coned by searchlights – but deBreyne managed to wriggle free and regain the comparative safety of the darkness. However, any security that they might have felt then was destined to be short-lived for when they were at 5,000ft and

*Wellington Mk III Z1572/*VR-Q *of No.419 (Moose) Squadron, Mildenhall, Suffolk. This aircraft was subsequently transferred to No.427 (Lion) Squadron, Croft, and was the aircraft in which Pilot Officer George Vandekerckhove earned his DFC on the night of 5/6 March, 1943. (see page 155) It was struck off charge on 30 April, 1945.* (Chas. E Brown)

settling lower towards their target, they were attacked from behind and below by a Ju88 nightfighter which straddled the Lancaster with cannon shells.

Three explosions rocked the bomber. Two shots knocked out both port engines and set a wing tank on fire. The third ripped into the fuselage, starting another fire between the mid-upper gun position and the rear turret. The Lancaster began to lose altitude and the pilot, realising the inevitability of the result, gave the order to bale out. The Lancaster threatened to spiral earthwards and so while deBreyne struggled to control the bomber long enough for his crew to escape, Friday, Vigars, Brodie and Kelly exited in that order through the nose hatch. When the pilot followed suit seconds later he believed that his gunners had also taken to their parachutes. But he was wrong: Brophy was trapped and Mynarski was attempting to free him.

*   *   *

The normal escape procedure for rear gunners required them to simply rotate their turret through 90 degrees and roll out backwards. Brophy, however, could not do that because his turret had jammed shortly after he had swung it to port to engage the fighter — and immediately after one of the cannon shells had destroyed the hydraulic system that powered his gun station. An added difficulty — though academic, given the lack of hydraulic power — was that he was not wearing his parachute: it was hanging inside the *fuselage*, out of his reach, and in the path of flames that were beginning to feed greedily on the fluid that was spilling from the ruptured pipes.

Mynarski was preparing to jump from the rear exit when he glimpsed his friend through the plexiglass panel. Recognising Brophy's

May 1945. No.428 (Ghost) Squadron Lancasters awaiting take-off from Middleton-St-George (via Chris Sheehan)

Pilot Officer Andrew Mynarski, No.419 (Moose) Squadron RCAF Middleton-St-George, whose efforts to save a crew mate on the night of 12 June, 1944, led to the posthumous award of the Victoria Cross. (DND/PL38261)

predicament, Mynarski ignored the flames that began to lick at his own clothing as he attempted to smash Brophy free with the aid of a fire axe. When that failed, he tore at the door with his bare hands — with an equal lack of success. By then his own clothing was ablaze from the waist down, and yet he continued to persist.

Brophy was the first to admit the futility of it all: he pleaded with Mynarski to leave while he still had the chance. It took several attempts but ultimately he was persuasive enough and, with reluctance, the would-be rescuer backed down the burning fuselage to the escape hatch, his clothing aflame and his gaze fixed on the rear gunner. On reaching the exit, he drew himself to attention, saluted his friend for the last time and was gone. Seconds later, the Lancaster touched earth close by the small village of Gaudiempré, near Amiens.

Contrary to the gunner's expectations, the fully-laden bomber hit the ground at a shallow angle, in the manner of crash-landing under pilot control. As the flaming hulk gouged its way across farm land the port wing struck a stout tree. The impact ripped away the mainplane, and wrenched open the rear turret. Brophy was hurled free: against all odds, he survived virtually unscathed.

But that was not so in the case of Andrew Mynarski. Frenchmen had watched his fiery descent and though he was alive when they reached him he was far beyond help and died shortly afterwards as a result of his severe burns. He now lies in the cemetery at Meharicourt, France.

When Brophy was able to tell his story, Andrew Mynarski was awarded

No.428 (Ghost) Squadron Lancasters marshalled for take-off from Middleton-St-George, May 1945 (Chris Sheehan)

171

a posthumous Victoria Cross. The citation that appeared in the *London Gazette* on 11 October, 1946, concludes:

'Pilot Officer Mynarski must have been fully aware that in trying to free the rear gunner he was almost certain to lose his own life. Despite this, with outstanding courage and complete disregard for his own safety, he went to the rescue. Willingly accepting danger, Pilot Officer Mynarski lost his life by a most conspicuous act of heroism which called for valour of the highest order.'

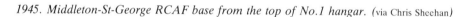

'We were scared when we went on an operation, at least I was, and I know I was not alone. Probably the worst time was after we got out to the aircraft and lined up for take off. We would get out and stand around, waiting until it was time to go, most had a cigarette or two and most had a nervous pee... Frankly, I did not expect to complete a tour of ops. The odds were all against finishing... We didn't really believe we would be around for long...'

[Ron Cassels: Navigator, No.428 (Ghost) Squadron, RCAF Middleton-St-George, 1944-45]

1945. Middleton-St-George RCAF base from the top of No.1 hangar. (via Chris Sheehan)

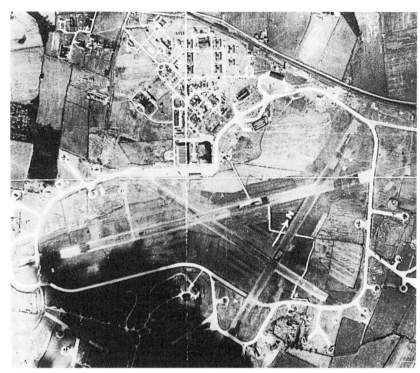

*3 March, 1944. Middleton-St-George from 8,000 feet. (*via Chris Sheehan*)*

30 December, 1944

There were times when Fate did smile kindly upon bomber crews, as Flying Officer 'Wimp' Noel and his crew [No.428 (Ghost) Squadron RCAF Middleton-St-George] discovered on the night of 30 December, 1944, when they flew Lancaster KB744/*NA-J* to Cologne's railway yards as part of an attacking force of 470 aircraft.

When Noel and his crew were some thirty minutes from the target, four anti-aircraft shells exploded just below their aircraft — their first encounter with a barrage which was to continue intermittently for a further nine minutes before the bomber finally broke free (the crew later learned that they had probably been engaged by anti-aircraft

Flying Officer Norman 'Wimp' Noel and his crew, No.428 (Ghost) Squadron RCAF, Middleton-St-George, line up in front of their regular aircraft Lancaster KB739/NA-Z, (L-R): Flight Sergeant Ron Cassels (navigator); Flight Sergeant Jack Watson (rear gunner); Sergeant Stuart Hanlin (flight engineer); Flying Officer Norman Noel (pilot); Warrant Officer 'Rodge' Rogers (wireless operator); Flight Sergeant Jack 'Mac' McKenzie (bomb aimer); Flight Sergeant Bill Carr (mid upper gunner). (Ron Cassels)

defences using proximity-fused shells which were detonated by the magnetism of the aircraft).

Due to damage, one engine had to be feathered, but Noel pressed on and bombed the target. The return trip was accomplished with some difficulty for control surfaces had also been damaged and the pilot had to wrestle with the aircraft for nearly four hours in order to make it back to base. Over England a second engine packed in and the rest of the flight was completed on two engines.

On arrival at Middleton-St-George, damage to the Lancaster's undercarriage caused further complications and required the pilot to land on only one wheel. Noel successfully managed to bring his aircraft down safely, but he could not prevent the ground-loop that followed.

Although the crash-landing further damaged *NA-J*, none of the occupants was injured. However, an examination of the aircraft the following morning revealed just how fortunate its crew had been. There were large holes in the wings and some of the trim tabs were missing: additionally, the starboard elevator had virtually disappeared and half of the rudder had gone. Shrapnel had punched some 160 holes through the fuselage but had missed every crew member: the area surrounding the rear turret 'had been peppered' but gunner Jack Watson was unharmed; there was a gaping hole ('several feet long and 3-4 feet

Early 1945. A newly-commissioned Ron Cassels sits astride a 4,000lb 'cookie' alongside Lancaster NA-U *at Middleton-St-George. Note the H2S blister below the mid-upper turret.* (Ron Cassels)

wide') in the fuselage floor where the H2s blister had been obliterated by flak, but Bill Carr, the mid-upper gunner who had been sitting directly above it, was unscathed; by tracking the path of at least one potentially lethal shard of metal, navigator Ron Cassels realised that 'a couple of bits of shrapnel had come through the floor between my feet, gone through the nav table and out through the top without me being aware', while flight engineer Stuart Hanlin had the cuff of his battle-dress cut but there was not even a scratch on his arm.

Ron Cassels who had a narrow escape over Cologne 30 December, 1944, when flying as a Flight Sergeant navigator of No.428 (Ghost) Squadron, Middleton-St-George.
(Ron Cassels)

NA-J never went on operations again, although it was repaired in time to fly back to Canada on 8 June, 1945. The crew it served well on the Cologne trip subsequently went on to complete their tour of operations in *Z-Zombie*, their usual aircraft.

Superstition

'*Flight Lieutenant Curtis and crew were doing the last trip (Dortmund, 12 September, 1944) of a second tour. Wattie, their navigator, was a rather superstitious type. When he came into the briefing room a new navigator on his first trip was sitting at the table usually used by Wattie. As Wattie passed by me he was swearing and I heard him mutter that they would get the chop for sure on their last trip. Realising what was bothering him, I went and asked the new navigator if he would find another table. I did not say anything to Wattie, who was busy emptying his nav bag. However, when he looked up and saw his table empty he immediately gathered up his charts and equipment and moved to his favourite table.*'

[Ron Cassels, ex-No.428 (Ghost) Squadron, in a letter to the writer, May 1994]

Postscript

In view of what subsequently happened, it is interesting to speculate whether Wattie's attitude towards such ritualistic behaviours was later modified. Their aircraft was hit by flak during its bombing run: the rear gunner was killed, the flight engineer was wounded, and Curtis suffered a compound fracture of his skull. The bomb-aimer, Pilot Officer McGillivary flew the aircraft back to England, where he made his first ever landing. Curtis subsequently recovered from his injuries and thus the crew, apart from the unfortunate rear gunner, completed their tour.

SEDGEFIELD
Co. Durham

On 24 November 1944, seven members of 419 (Moose) Squadron, Middleton-St-George, were killed when their Lancaster (KB785/VR-Y) caught fire while on a training flight and crashed at Sands Hall Farm, Bradbury, near Sedgefield, Co. Durham. The crew was as follows: F/O Richard Mansfield DFC (pilot); P/O George Warren-Darley (navigator); F/O Alan Hurst (bomb aimer); P/O Derrick Newland (flight engineer); F/Sgt Douglas Gunn (wireless operator); F/Sgt Leslie Toth (mid-upper gunner); and John Murphy (rear gunner).

Sedgefield resident Betty Amlin, whose husband had served with the squadron and who had long been aware of the tragedy, felt that the fiftieth anniversary of the incident should not pass unnoticed. She approached the local council with a view to organising a commemorative event and they agreed to have a plaque dedicated.

The slate tablet, which is set in the wall alongside the War Memorial, was unveiled on Sunday 19 June 1994 following a church service conducted by the Rector and Rural Dean of Sedgefield, the Rev. Martin King. Some three hundred people, including veterans, Canadian relatives of the Lancaster crew and many villagers, gathered on the green to witness the event. Dignitaries included the Mayor of Sedgefield, Cllr John Robinson; Cllr Jim Wayman, chairman of the organising committee; Colonel John David, Canadian Air Force advisor to the Canadian High Commission, London; and Lt. Colonel JP McNeil, the current Commanding Officer of 419 (Moose) Squadron.

Prior to the service of dedication and rememberance, squadron veterans—led by the Newton Aycliffe Pipe Band—paraded to the site in the company of a guard of honour from the present 419 (Moose) Squadron (flown over from their base in Cold Lake, Alberta); a contingent from RAF Leeming, and members of the Air Training Corps.

The unveiling was carried out by Mrs Mildred Warren-Darley (widow of the Lancaster's navigator), assisted by Cllr Robinson; the dedication was performed by Canon Norman Edmonson, RAF Chaplain and a former Rector of Sedgefield.

A flypast by four F18s of the Canadian Air Force brought the occasion to a dramatic conclusion, the four aircraft flying over the cenotaph twice in close formation before each executed a solo low run over the site and then climbed spectacularly to disappear into the cloud high above.

After the conclusion of the ceremony, a maple tree donated by Mr and Mrs Amlin was planted at the roadside by Beaver, Brownie, Cub and Guide groups.

No.424 (Tiger) Squadron and No.433 (Porcupine) Squadron, RCAF

SKIPTON-ON-SWALE

'No matter how disparate our backgrounds, there is a bond forged forever when you face death night after night and depend on the skills and courage of your crew mates. That professional skill and, above all, courage, was not lacking in any way in our crew.'

Jim Kinder, ex-Flying Officer (navigator),
No.433 Squadron RCAF, Skipton-on-Swale 1944

Skipton-on-Swale (North Yorkshire) aerodrome was opened in the Autumn of 1942 as a satellite of RAF Leeming and was transferred to No.6 (RCAF) Group in January 1943. Canadian squadrons Nos.420 and 432 both had short postings there, but the base is more closely identified with No.433 (Porcupine) Squadron, which formed there in September 1943, and No.424 (Tiger) Squadron, which arrived two months later after a short spell of service in North Africa.

A Lancaster Mk I of No.424 (Tiger) Squadron RCAF Skipton-on-Swale (DND/PL44204)

*Halifax Mk II (MZ910) of No.433 (Porcupine) Squadron, Skipton-on-Swale. This aircraft completed thirty-two operational sorties before being shot down over Witten, in the Ruhr, on 19 March, 1945. (*Yorkshire Air Museum*)*

Flying Halifax BIIIs until January 1945, when they converted to Lancaster Is and IIIs, both squadrons operated from Skipton until the cessation of hostilities. During that time they participated in almost every major raid launched against Germany and Occupied Europe.

By the end of the war, No.424 Squadron had flown on 235 raids and carried out of 2,531 sorties in the European theatre of operations since its formation at Topcliffe in October 1942. Sixty-one of its members had been decorated, but thirty-three (1.3 percent) aircraft had been lost and a further two (Lancasters) had been destroyed in crashes.[1]

Members of No.433 Squadron were awarded 160 decorations during 2,316 operational sorties carried out at a cost of thirty-six aircraft lost (including five in non-operational incidents)[2] and 241 personnel killed or missing; non-operational casualties accounted for a further thirteen aircrew and two ground crew. One such tragedy is recorded on the Skipton-on-Swale memorial.

1. HALPENNY (1982) gives the total sorties as 3,257 (including 668 from North Africa), with fifty-two aircraft lost and 313 crew killed or missing. CASSELS (1991) puts the number of sorties at 3,218 and claims the number of aircraft lost as fifty-six, which includes four destroyed in non-operational incidents.

2. HALPENNY (1982) puts the non-operational losses at seven aircraft. CASSELS (1991) confirms the total loss of thirty-eight aircraft but claims that all were due to operations.

179

5 August, 1944

The simple monument of Halifax stone that stands on the village green records that two fliers and one civilian lost their lives in August 1944, when a disabled Royal Canadian Air Force bomber crashed there on its return from operations.

The aircraft was a Halifax BIII (*BM-H*; MZ828) of No.433 (Porcupine) Squadron, RCAF, and was crewed by: Flying Officer Jimmy Harrison (pilot); Flight Sergeant Dennis Whitbread RAF (flight engineer); Flying Officer Jim Kinder (navigator); Flying Officer Edwin Widenoja (bomb-aimer); Flying Officer Laurent Dufresne (wireless operator); Flight Sergeant Alan Bourne (mid-upper gunner); and Pilot Officer NS Godfrey RAF (rear gunner).

Harrison's crew had joined No.433 Squadron in April 1944, when the squadron was becoming increasingly involved in Bomber Command's 'tactical phase' in preparation for the Normandy landings. By D-Day, they had flown seventeen operations and were considered to be veterans.

On 5 August, 1944, Bomber Command detailed 742 aircraft to attack flying-bomb storage sites at Foret de Nieppe and St-Leu-d'Esserant: Harrison's men were among the nineteen crews from No.433 Squadron briefed to raid the latter.

Flying Officer James R Harrison, pilot of No.433 Squadron (RCAF) Halifax Mk III (MZ828) which crashed at Skipton-on-Swale, 5 August, 1944.

On that occasion they were without their usual 'tail-end Charlie'. Godfrey was a 'spare', the regular rear gunner, Sergeant Ray Beaudette, having been temporarily excused duties. In early June, he and Harrison had been involved in a motorcycle accident. Beaudette had suffered spinal injuries from which he had not yet fully recovered; his pilot had suffered a broken ankle. Harrison had resumed flying only the day before, when he had piloted his Halifax in a daylight raid on the flying-bomb site at Bois de Cassan. Given what was to follow, it is interesting to speculate whether Jim Harrison had returned to duties too early.

180

Jim Kinder recalls:

'... on the way to dispersal Jim Harrison changed aircraft with a pilot named Miller. In their discussion, Jim said that our assigned aircraft had difficult rudder controls and that his injured ankle was still giving him trouble. Miller offered to exchange aircraft and we ended up with *BM-H*, designated 'Harry'...

We took off at 1040 hours and arrived over the target area at approx. 1300 hrs. We experienced no problems on the way. The weather was fair with small amounts of cumulus cloud. Certainly no problems with visibility. On our approach to the target there appeared to be heavy flak (Intelligence had said we could expect little). It was predicted (which means it was being controlled by radar) and it was accurate. Other aircraft seemed to be having trouble with the flak. One, on our altitude and flying approximately 150 yards in front of us, was hit and lost their starboard wing. We did not see anyone get out.

We didn't escape. We were hit and lost our outer starboard engine. It stopped and Jim 'feathered' the prop. All of us did a visual check for other damage, but there didn't seem to be any. Dennis Whitbread confirmed that the only damage seemed to be the starboard outer engine.'

A more thorough check subsequently undertaken by the pilot and his

Jimmy Harrison's crew pose in front of a Halifax bomber.
FRONT (L-R): Ed. Widenoja (bomb-aimer); Jim Kinder (navigator); Jim Harrison (pilot).
BACK (L-R): Dennis Whitbread (flight engineer); Ray Beaudette (rear gunner); Al Bourne (mid-upper gunner); Laurent Dufresne (wireless operator). (J Kinder)

Four members of Jimmy Harrison's crew pose alongside Halifax BM-A.
L-R: *Dennis Whitbread (flight engineer); Ray Beaudette (rear gunner); Al Bourne (mid-upper gunner) and Ed Widenoja (bomb aimer).* (Laurent Dufresne)

engineer showed the three remaining engines to be operating normally, all systems in order, and no structural damage.

On orders from Group HQ, the Squadron returned to base in formation, with *BM-H* seemingly having no difficulty keeping up. The first sign of trouble occurred over Goole, 50 miles from base, when 'engine problems' forced Harrison to drop out of formation. Shortly before his arrival at Skipton, he was having trouble maintaining power in the three remaining engines and was granted priority landing.

Established procedure laid down crew positions for landing: the bomb-aimer in the (right-hand) co-pilot's seat; the flight engineer standing directly behind the pilot; the other crew members at designated stations within the fuselage. The crew were at their stations when their aircraft made its approach from the north-west.

As the Halifax was eased towards the runway, Harrison experienced difficulty lining up with the tarmac. Whether this was due to the persistent lack of power from his remaining engines — and especially the starboard inner − or because his injured ankle '...was still giving him trouble...' may be a matter of conjecture. Whatever the reason, some 200 feet above the airfield he decided to abort his first attempt and go round again. His expected flightpath would take him *east* of Skipton village.

Laurent Dufresne remembers that:

'My position as we came in to land was sitting on the bench in the middle of the fuselage. I had my intercom plugged in and heard the pilot give the order for wheels up and *flaps up* when he decided to go round again.'

However, although the undercarriage was raised as Harrison attempted to climb away, his flaps stayed *down*. It is not known whether the pilot was aware of this situation, but it became necessary to use full power (eventually going 'through the gate') in an attempt to gain height. Jim Kinder believes that the starboard inner engine then failed just as the Halifax was at stalling speed. The combination of full throttle and slow speed caused the bomber to bank steeply to starboard and turn through 270 degrees in an uncontrollable manoeuvre that brought it low over the village. Harrison must have realized then that he did not have enough power to make a landing and that they were going to crash because he ordered Widenoja to 'jump' (ie dive into the fuselage).

The violent lurch to starboard had catapulted Laurent Dufresne to the other side of the fuselage, where, through a port hole, he had caught a glimpse of trees and houses very close. He just had time to throw himself into his crash position before 'Ed' dived on top of him. The crash came seconds later.

Approaching low from the south-east, the Halifax brushed tree tops on the edge of the village and clipped the corner of Skipton Hall before dropping on to the very large elm tree that had stood for centuries on the small village green. Skipton farmer Maurice Sanderson, who witnessed the crash as a 15-year-old schoolboy, maintains that the elm virtually stopped the Halifax in its tracks and thus prevented a number of civilian casualties. The plane broke up on impact. Much of the wreckage stayed close by the tree, but the momentum propelled forward some separating parts of fuselage until they came to rest against a wall of cottages at the crossroads.

The crash claimed the lives of Jim Harrison and Dennis Whitbread; the rest of the crew survived, though for some the extent of their injuries would require months of hospitalization. Five weeks were to pass before Jim Kinder was able to visit the Squadron. It was then that he learned that the crash had claimed a further victim: 5-year-old Kenneth Battensby, who had been playing in a nearby garden when he was killed by flying debris.

The wreckage of No.433 Squadron Halifax BM-H *(MZ828), showing the elm tree and the telephone box occupied by Ray Beaudette.* (J Kinder)

An interesting sidelight to the crash is that Ray Beaudette, the gunner that they had left behind, was at the site when the aircraft hit. He was standing by the telephone-box close by the elm tree and waiting for an ambulance to take him to the Friarage Hospital in Northallerton. When he saw the plane coming and apparently going to crash, he made a speedy getaway. But when the scene settled and he realized that his own crew were involved he went into shock. The ambulance that he finally travelled in also carried his crew-mates!

In 1982, ex-members of Nos.424 and 433 Squadrons RCAF who had served at the airfield made contact with Maurice Sanderson, the current owner of the site, who farms it as his family has done for generations. At their invitation he attended their 1982 annual reunion in Toronto as an honoured guest. The giant tree had succumbed to Dutch elm disease the year before and the visit provided an opportunity to make a plea for a Canadian maple to take its place on the village green to remind future generations of the sacrifices made during the Second World War. It soon became clear that a tree by itself would mean little and thus in addition it was decided to erect a cairn to incorporate a plaque to honour the four RCAF squadrons which had served at Skipton during the Second World War. Subscriptions were raised by the Memorial Committee in Canada; the English committee – consisting of Maurice Sanderson, ex-No.433 members Fred Haynes and Ron Reinelt, and Harrogate RAFA member Les Cardall – were responsible for the local arrangements.

The memorial cairn, made, appropriately, from Halifax stone, was erected alongside the maple, close to the site once occupied by the old elm tree. It was unveiled by Kenneth Battensby's brother on 19 May, 1984, in the presence of Jim Harrison's brother and Dennis Whitbread's sister, during a service conducted by the Reverend W Smith, Rector of St John's Parish Church, Skipton-on-Swale, and the Reverend P Cooper, RAF (Ret'd) Padre, Skipton-on-Swale. The service was attended by over 200 former RCAF personnel and their families, as well as a large number of the general public. The RAF was represented by Air Marshal Sir Leslie Mavor, KCB AFC and Group Captain DG Curry, CO RAF Leeming. Canadian representatives included Mr D Jamieson, High Commissioner for Canada; Wing Commander C Sinton DFC, wartime CO of No.433 Squadron, Skipton-on-Swale; and Lieutenant-Colonel JE Boyle and Colonel CD Coffen, the then current commanding officers of Nos.433 Squadron and 424 Squadron respectively. The civic authorities were represented by the mayors of Thirsk and Harrogate. Also among the congregation were Ray Beaudette, Al Bourne, Laurent Dufresne and Jim Kinder, for whom the occasion had its own special meaning. The Lancaster bomber of the RAF Memorial Flight provided the flypast.

May 1995, site of the Skipton-on-Swale Halifax crash. The memorial stands to the left of the white house.

(L-R): *Alan Bourne, Laurent Dufresne, Jim Kinder and Ray Beaudette chat with Alice Meggit whose cottage was damaged when it was struck by the tail unit of the Halifax. Taken at the unveiling of the Skipton-on-Swale memorial, 19 May, 1984.* (Northern Echo)

The dedication of the RCAF memorial cairn, Skipton-on-Swale, 19 May, 1984. The cairn stands on the site of the elm with which the Halifax collided; the telephone-box occupied by Ray Beaudette at the time of the crash can be seen to the left of the monument. (Northern Echo)

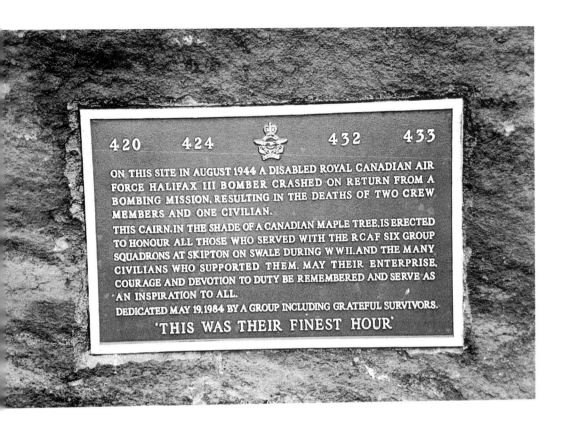

On this site in August 1944 a disabled Royal Canadian Air Force Halifax III bomber crashed on return from a bombing mission, resulting in the deaths of two crew members and one civilian.

This cairn, in the shade of a Canadian Maple Tree, is erected to honour all those who served with the RCAF Six Group Squadrons at Skipton on Swale during WWII, and the many civilians who supported them. May their enterprise, courage and devotion to duty be remembered and serve as an inspiration to all.

Dedicated May 19, 1984 by a group including grateful survivors.

'THIS WAS THEIR FINEST HOUR'

Superstition

'One symptom of our reaction to the strain of operations was that we became increasingly unwilling to change anything. We had to urinate on the tail wheel in exactly the same order before every flight, file into the aircraft in the same way, go through the same airborne ritual every time in exactly the same way. Linklater (pilot) and Ron (flight engineer) went through their pre-take off checks in the same way, like priests readying themselves for an airborne Mass, with every motion ritually correct... We did not want to do anything that might change our luck.

And once, after I had climbed aboard the aircraft and settled down, with my maps thumb-tacked to the navigation table, Linklater called up to say, "What do you always say just before we get into the kite?"

"Once more into the breach, dear friends."

"Well, damn it, this time you didn't say it. Get out there and say it and then get back aboard again."

I complied. After all, for all I knew it was that magic phrase that so far kept us reasonably safe from harm.'

[Norman Emmott, ex-navigator, No.433 (Porcupine) Squadron RCAF]

No.429 (Bison) Squadron, No.432 (Leaside) Squadron and No.415 (Swordfish) Squadron, RCAF

SUTTON ON THE FOREST

Eastmoor aerodrome, close by the Yorkshire village of Sutton on the Forest, was opened on 1 June, 1942, as part of No.4 Group, Bomber Command. The first unit to be based there was No.158 Squadron, who moved in on 7 June, 1942. However, they were not destined to stay long and during the first week of the following November they moved to Rufforth (and later to Lissett) to be replaced by No.429 (Bison) Squadron RCAF, the first squadron to begin Eastmoor's association with the Canadians which was to last until the end of the war.

No.429 (Bison) Squadron was formed at Eastmoor as part of No.4 Group on 7 November, 1942, and was equipped with the Wellington Mk III until the following January, when the Mk X version was introduced. The Squadron transferred to No.6 (RCAF) Group on 1 April, 1943. Their move to Leeming, in August 1943, coincided with conversion to the Halifax Mk II, a type that they operated for three months before being assigned the Halifax Mk V. During the Second World War No.429 (Bison) Squadron flew a total of 3175 sorties in 267 operations and lost 78 (2.5%) aircraft.[1]

No.432 (Leaside) Squadron arrived at Eastmoor on 19 September, 1943, having formed at Skipton-on-Swale the previous May. Initially equipped with Wellington Mk X, the Squadron converted to the Lancaster Mk II in October 1943. Two other changes of aircraft were to follow: to the Halifax Mk III (February 1944) and then to the Halifax Mk VII (July 1944), the latter being retained until the end of hostilities. The Squadron flew its first operation – to Dortmund – on 23/24 May, 1943, and its last – to attack gun positions on the island of Wangerooge – on 25 April, 1945. In between, it flew 3128 sorties (including fifty-three sea mining) in 246 operations at a cost of seventy-three aircraft (2.3 percent) and 448 aircrew, 290 of whom were killed or presumed dead. Of the rest, 123 were made prisoners of war and thirty-five managed to evade capture. Non-operational casualties amounted to forty-two, of whom thirty-eight were killed. 144 decorations were awarded to Squadron personnel: two DSOs, one Bar to DFC, 119 DFCs, one CGM, twenty DFMs and one Croix de Guerre (France) lost. The Squadron disbanded at Eastmoor on 15 March, 1945.[2]

No.415 (Swordfish) Squadron formed at Thorney Island as a Coastal

Command Torpedo-bomber Squadron on 20 August, 1941, and served at St Eval, North Coates, Wick, Tain, Leuchars and Bircham Newton before being transferred to Bomber Command in July 1944. The Squadron arrived at Eastmoor on 26 July, 1944, and converted from the Albacore to the Halifax Mk III, a type they continued to operate until they were allocated the Mk VII version in March 1945. They flew their first bomber operation on the night of 28/29 July, when they detailed sixteen Halifaxes for an attack on Hamburg: one aircraft crashed on take-off; another failed to return. Their last operation took place on 25 April, 1945, when they despatched eighteen aircraft to bomb gun emplacements on the East Frisian island of Wangerooge.

According to *The Bomber Command War Diaries* (1990 ed.), the Squadron flew 1,526 Halifax sorties on 104 bombing raids and lost 13 (0.9 percent) aircraft, but these figures are disputed.[3]

Early in 1988 individual Canadians from the three squadrons began to consider the need for a memorial to those who had served at Eastmoor and who had failed to return. While possible sites were being surveyed, the Parish Council at Sutton on the Forest offered a small plot of land (known locally as 'The Pound') in the village, and a memorial fund was launched in September 1988. Committees were formed on both sides of the Atlantic, each with representatives from the three squadrons.

The Eastmoor memorial consists of a sundial of black slate set into a plinth of green Westmorland slate standing on a slab of Yorkshire stone. The plinth bears the crest of RCAF on one side, with each of the other sides engraved with the badge of one of the three squadrons. − Nos.429, 432, 415

*The Eastmoor memorial service, Sutton-on-the-Forest, 2 June, 1990 (*Yorkshire Evening Press*)*

It was unveiled on 2 June, 1990, by Squadron Leader WER 'Danny' Boone (the first Engineering Officer of No.432 Squadron), assisted by Wing Commander 'Art' McKay and Squadron Leader Clive Sinton (the first Flight Commanders of No.432 Squadron), during a ceremony attended by some 300 people (including many Canadians). Invited guests included members of the Parish Council; the Mayor and Mayoress of Bradford, whose city had adopted No.429 Squadron during the war; and a Canadian Air Force representative from the Canadian High Commission Defence Liaison Staff, London. The Royal Air Force was represented by Air Marshal Sir Leslie Mavor, KCB AFC OStJ FRAeS DL, who also took the salute. The memorial was dedicated by the Reverend T McCoulough, Vicar of All Hallows Church, Sutton-on-the-Forest, following the Address which was delivered by Father Harry Schmuck, an ex-No.432 Squadron rear-gunner.

The monument bears the inscription as follows:

This memorial is dedicated to all who served at Eastmoor in World War II, many of whom gave their lives, and in gratitude to the people of Yorkshire who welcomed them.

Erected by their families and former colleagues.

Dedicated this 2nd day of June 1990.

1. HALPENNY (1982) gives the figures for No.429 Squadron as 3,221 sorties carried out and seventy-one aircraft lost. Crew losses are given as 451, made up of eighty-two killed, 322 missing, twenty-three prisoners of war and twenty-four safe. Awards are listed as: forty-five DFCs; two Bars to DFC; one AFC; one CGM; and seven DFMs. CASSELS (1991) states operational losses in aircraft as being seventy-one but he adds eleven for losses on no-operational duties, thus raising the total figure to 82.

2. No.432 (Leaside) Squadron details provided by Ivan Mulley, Secretary of *The Eastmoor Family*. *Bomber Command War Diaries* (1990) gives 3,100 sorties in 230 raids (including twenty-nine mine-laying) for a loss of sixty-five (2.1 percent) aircraft.

3. HALPENNY (1982) gives the figures as 1,608 bomber sorties, with losses of twenty-two (1.4 percent) aircraft and 151 aircrew (an unknown number of which were made POWs).

21 August, 1944

In the afternoon of 21 August, 1944, No.415 (Swordfish) Squadron RCAF Eastmoor lost two veteran aircrews during a routine transit flight.

Earlier in the day both crews, skippered by Wing Commander JG McNeill DFC (Squadron Commanding Officer) and Squadron Leader BE Wilmot DFC ('A' Flight Commander), had flown to Exeter in Halifax Mk III NA609 to collect another No.415 Squadron Halifax (MZ633) which had undergone an engine change there. A total of twelve aircrew and thirteen ground personnel (of the Squadron's Servicing Wing) were aboard the two aircraft when they returned north in close formation in the late afternoon.

As they neared Eastmoor, the crews were heard by Flying Control communicating with each other; disaster struck minutes later. It is believed that when the bombers were approaching Selby, the starboard inner propeller broke off NA609, causing it to swing into the other aircraft.

No-one survived the collision. Eye-witnesses at RAF station Burn subsequently stated that the aircraft were in pieces and on fire when they broke cloud; wreckage was scattered over a wide area and fell between the villages of Birkin and West Haddsley, which lie to the south-west of Selby.

Sadly, the names of the ground personnel who died in the crash are not known, but the following aircrew lost their lives in the incident and were buried in Stonefall Cemetery, Harrogate:

Wing Commander	JG McNeill DFC	pilot (Squadron CO)
Flight Lieutenant	G Steel-Davis	navigator
Flying Officer	FH Bain	bomb-aimer
Sergeant	WH Fox	wireless operator
Sergeant	AW Mitchell	air gunner
Sergeant	TC Guthrie	flight engineer
Squadron Leader	BE Wilmot DFC	pilot ('A' Flight Commander)
Flying Officer	JA Hudson	navigator
Pilot Officer	TE Wiltse	bomb-aimer
Flight Lieutenant	W Eagleston	wireless operator
Sergeant	RC Morrison	air gunner
Sergeant	ML Malpasse	flight engineer

ALDBOROUGH, nr BOROUGHBRIDGE

Lancaster BII LL686/*QO-F* of No.432 (Leaside) Squadron, RCAF crashed at Aldborough, near Boroughbridge, on the night of 2 February 1944. The bomber had left its base at Eastmoor on a night training flight and had burst into flames shortly before crashing at Studforth Hill, on the southern edge of the village. The crew of the seven were killed: their average age was twenty-one years.

Fifty years later, the villagers of Aldborough erected a plaque to the memory of the crew. It was unveiled on Sunday, 11 December 1994 and is located on the wall of the old courthouse that overlooks the village green.

No.420 (Snowy Owl) Squadron, No.425 (Alouette) Squadron, No.431 (Iroquois) Squadron and No.434 (Bluenose) Squadron, RCAF

THOLTHORPE

The North Yorkshire village of Tholthorpe, set between the A1 and the A19, lies almost mid-way between Boroughbridge and Easingwold. The memorial that stands close by the pond on the green commemorates the Canadians who served at the nearby aerodrome from 1943 to 1945.

Opened in August, 1940, as a grass aerodrome and satellite for Linton-on-Ouse, Tholthorpe served as a base for the Mk V Whitleys of No.77 Squadron RAF until the following December, when it was closed to allow conversion to a heavy bomber station.

Re-opened in July, 1943, as part of No.6 Group RCAF, the airfield was the first home of No.434 (Bluenose) Squadron, RCAF, which formed there during the same month; No.431 (Iroquois) Squadron followed some four weeks later. Both squadrons operated their Halifax B Mk Vs from Tholthorpe until December, 1943, when they moved northwards to Croft.

They were replaced by No.420 (Snowy Owl) and No.425 (Alouette) squadrons and both were operational by mid-February, 1944, following conversion to Halifax B Mk III aircraft. They operated from Tholthorpe for the remainder of the war, returning to Canada in June 1945, prior to their disbandment in Nova Scotia in the following September. During their stay, both squadrons took part in raids against a number of major targets in Germany as well as supporting the Normandy invasion and participating in attacks against flying-bomb sites.

RCAF Memorial, Tholthorpe

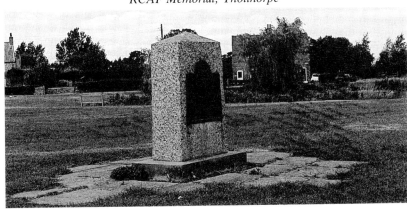

No.420 Squadron had flown Hampden light-bombers following its formation at Waddington, Lincolnshire, as part of No.5 Group in December 1941. In August 1942, the Squadron was transferred to No.4 Group and was re-located to Skipton-on-Swale, the move northwards coinciding with conversion to Wellingon Mk IIIs. In the following February these were discarded in favour of the Mk X version. On 16 October 1942 the squadron moved to Middleton-St-George and in the following May was posted to the Middle East for a six month tour of duty. On its return (November 1943), No.420 stayed at Dalton for one month before moving to Tholthorpe – its home for the remainder of the war – and converting to the Halifax Mk III. During its operational service, No.420 (Snowy Owl) Squadron carried out a total of 3,479 sorties in 314 raids and lost sixty (1.7 percent) aircraft; during its Yorkshire-based operations the Squadron flew 2,944 sorties in 224 raids and lost forty-one aircraft.[1] Squadron personnel were awarded thirty-eight DFCs, one Bar to the DFC, and nine DFMs.

No.425 (Alouette) Squadron, RCAF, was the fifth Canadian squadron – and the first French-Canadian unit – to be formed overseas. It was established at Dishforth on 25 June, 1942, as part of No.4 Group Bomber Command but was transferred to No.6 (RCAF) Group in the first month of the new year. It operated Wellington Mk IIIs from August 1942 until the following April, when it re-equipped with the Mk X version. The Squadron was posted to North Africa on 16 May, 1943, returning to Dishforth six months later (6 November). Its stay there was destined to be a short one for on 10 December, 1943, No.425 (Alouette) Squadron severed its ties with Dishforth and moved to Tholthorpe preparatory to converting to Halifax Mk IIIs.

No.425 (Alouette) Squadron carried out its first operation – and sustained its first casualties – on the night of 5/6 October 1942, when eight of its Wellingtons formed part of a force of 257 aircraft launched against Aachen. Ten aircraft (3.9 percent) failed to return from that operation. The Alouettes lost one Wellington (X3843/*KW-G*), which plunged to earth near Debden (Essex) while en route to the target. The five-man crew – Sergeant MF O'Driscoll, Sergeant JB Sandiford, Sergeant T Howells, Sergeant JM Armstrong and Flight Sergeant AC Challis – perished in the crash. During the period of its service with Nos.4 and 6 Groups, No.425 (Alouette) Squadron launched 225 raids (2,927 sorties) at a cost of thirty-nine (1.3 percent) aircraft lost and its members were awarded 190 decorations, with four Mentions in Despatches.[2]

1. CASSELS (1991) very probably takes into account No.420s Middle East operations when he gives the number of sorties as 4,186. He also lists operational losses as sixty-five with a further three aircraft being destroyed in non-operational incidents. HALPENNY (1982) agrees CASSELS' losses and gives losses of personnel attributable to operations as 324 aircrew, of whom 312 were killed or missing; twelve personnel were killed on non-operational duties.

2. HALPENNY (1982) very probably takes into account No.425s Middle East operations when he puts the number of sorties as 3,665 sorties in 287 raids, with fifty-five aircraft failing to return; a further eleven are listed as being lost in non-operational incidents. Casualties listed include operational losses of 338 aircrew, of whom 190 are shown as killed or missing, and non-operational losses of sixty-four killed. CASSELS (1991) agrees with HALPENNY'S losses of aircraft but gives the number of sorties as 3,694

7 June, 1986. Air Vice Marshal Donald Bennett CB, CBE, DSO, FRAeS, founder of the wartime Pathfinder Force, talks to veterans after unveiling the Tholthorpe memorial. (David E. Thompson)

The Tholthorpe monument exists partly because of the efforts of local farmer Geoff Wood, who was ten years old when the Canadians arrived in the village for the first time — some of them to be billeted at the Woods' Manor Farm. The son of a First World War flier, and a boy who had '...always been keen on aircraft...', his interest in Tholthorpe aerodrome was immediate and has never waned.

In 1983, he established contact with the RCAF Allied Forces Reunion (an Old Comrades association) who were preparing to specially honour the four Tholthorpe squadrons in Toronto in October of that year. He accepted an invitation to attend the reunion and it was there that he suggested the erection of a memorial in the village. Committees were formed in Canada (chaired by ex-425 pilot Bert Milliken) and in Tholthorpe (led by Geoff) and their combined efforts came to fruition on 7 June, 1986, when the memorial was unveiled by ex-Pathfinder leader Air Vice-Marshal Donald Bennett watched by some 350 Canadians (including relatives) who had journeyed across the Atlantic for the occasion.

The granite memorial stands as testament to man's sacrifice, but, perhaps, a more poignant reminder is to be found on the site of the aerodrome, a mile or so to the east and linked to the village by a narrow road flanked by English oaks and Canadian maples. Most of the buildings that once occupied the field have long since disappeared; the few that remain are glimpsed behind climbing foliage, inevitably succumbing to Nature's inexorable camouflage.

The tower is the exception. Inhabited now by pigeons and (in July

1991) families of house-martins, its rooms littered with agricultural debris and spent plastic bags labelled *Nitro Top* the squat, derelict block has become a memorial of numerous impermanent inscriptions, impulsively scored into the rendering by men who once served there and who have felt the need to return and to remember.

Some of the scratchings merely record names: ... *Bing Reid, 420 WOP/AG... Cecil Davies, F/L 425...* a visitors' book set in plaster. Others bear witness to friends lost in a different age, but the memory of whom has met Time's test: ...*In memory of Sgt W. Gracie, killed 5.8.44...In memory of F. Trimby 434...F/O Stu Hunt 425 ..F/O C. Fox RCAF 420. We will always remember them.*

In July 1991, in spite of the intrusions of overflying Provosts from nearby Linton-on-Ouse, Tholthorpe tower had its own cast of evocative quiet: a combination of sighing grain stirring in the light breeze and, perhaps, thoughts of ghosts that one imagines to be there. Many of those commemorated by the granite memorial on the green laid down their lives far from the old bomber base. Thus it is fitting that in July of each passing year the yellowing acres of ripening wheat are flecked with the sprinkled scarlet of poppies.

'...*a visitors book set in plaster...*' Tholthorpe control tower, July 1991

PLACE OF GHOSTS

Listen...listen...can you hear?
That whispered sound, so very slight,
And feel again a long shed fear,
As day gives way to moonless night.

See, beyond those misted trees,
Weed choked and crazed, our ruined bay,
Where power surged, on nightly breeze
And I hear again, this fading day.

Surely I am not alone
To sense and feel the pulsing air;
Now a rising, higher tone
And look...I see them...over there...

Shadows, tipped in red and green,
I count them as they pass me by;
Numbers more than ever seen,
Myriad pin-points drench the sky.

Can't you hear...Don't you see?
Think, and you will understand;
These sounds and sights can only be
The Passing of the Lost Command.

Rex Polendine

Tholthorpe control tower, July 1991

No.425 was a French-Canadian squadron and thus the Tholthorpe monument bears inscriptions in French and in English, one on each side of the memorial. Each inscription appears on a bronze plaque and is surmounted by the RCAF crest. To ensure that the sun shines for an equal length of time on each side, the memorial is aligned along the North-South axis.

Inscriptions:

420   431
SNOWY OWL   IROQUOIS
THIS MONUMENT OF CANADIAN GRANITE AND THE AVENUE OF
OAKS AND MAPLES BETWEEN THIS VILLAGE AND THE OLD AERODROME
ARE, WITH HONOURED REMEMBRANCE TO THEIR
FALLEN COMRADES, A MEMORIAL TO THOSE WHO SERVED IN THESE
ROYAL CANADIAN AIR FORCE
SQUADRONS, TO THE STATION STAFF AT THOLTHORPE DURING THE
SECOND WORLD WAR, AND TO THE MANY CITIZENS OF THIS
COMMUNITY WHO SUPPORTED THEM. MAY THEIR COURAGE AND
DEVOTION TO DUTY IN THE CAUSE OF FREEDOM, EVER BE
REMEMBERED. DEDICATED BY THE PEOPLE OF THOLTHORPE AND
THE SURVIVING VETERANS, JUNE 7 1986

434   425
BLUENOSE   ALOUETTE

425   434
ALOUETTE   BLUENOSE
CE MONUMENT DE GRANIT CANADIEN ET L'AVENUE BORDEE
D'ERABLES
ET DE CHENES RELIANT CE VILLAGE A L'ACIEN AERODROME SONT
DEDIES AUX AVIATEURS QUI ONT FAIT LE SACRIFICE DE LEUR VIE
AINSI QU'A TOUS CEUX QUI ONT SERVI, DURANT LA SECONDE GUERRE
MONDIALE, DANS CE QUATRE
ESCADRILLES DE L'AVIATION
ROYALE DU CANADA
L'ON VEUT AUSSI HONORER LE PERSONNEL NON NAVISANT DE LA BASE
DE THOLTHORPE ET LES NOMBREUX CITOYENS DE CETTE
LOCALITE POUR LEUR LOYAL SOUTIEN. PUISSONS-NOUS NE
JAMAIS OUBLIER LEUR COURAGE ET LEUR DEVOUEMENT POUR LA
CAUSE DE LA LIBERTE. DEDIE PAR LES MEMBRES SURVIVANTS
ET LES CITOYENS DE THOLTHORPE EN CE 7 JOUR DE JUIN 1986.

431   420
IROQUOIS   SNOWY OWL

26/27 June 1944

Attacks on enemy-held territory were always dangerous – but there were also times when life on the station brought its own perils. One such occasion occurred in the summer of 1944.

On the night of 26/27 June of that year Tholthorpe Halifaxes bombed the V-1 sites at Foret d'Eawy. One of the aircraft taking part was Halifax *KW-A* of No.425 Squadron, which returned to base on three engines. On landing, it collided with an aircraft (*KW-U*) of the same squadron which was already bombed-up and waiting in dispersal. Both machines erupted in flames. Ignoring the intense heat and the serious risk of explosions, Air Commodore AD Ross, Flight Sergeant JRM St. Germain and Corporal Marquet – assisted by LACs M. McKenzie and R. Wolfe – went to the aid of the seriously injured pilot and the tail-gunner of the returning Halifax. They succeeded in rescuing both, in spite of twice being flattened by explosions of 500lb bombs in the second aircraft.

Air Vice-Marshal Clifford Mackay 'Black Mike' McEwan, Officer Commanding No.6 (RCAF) Group in 1944 congratulates No.425 Squadron personnel who took part in the rescue at Tholthorpe on the night of 26/27 June, 1944.
(Left-Right): Air Vice-Marshal McEwan, Flight Sergeant St. Germain, Leading Air Craftsman M. McKenzie, and Corporal M Marquet. (DND/PL33961)

Debris from the second blast virtually severed one of Ross's wrists, which was subsequently amputated. Their bravery was later acknowledged by the award of the George Cross to Ross and the George Medal to each of his helpers.

4 November, 1944

Bomber Command's primary target for the night of 4 November, 1944, was the important coal and steel producing centre of Bochum, in the heart of the Ruhr. Of the 749 aircraft despatched, twenty-eight (3.7 percent) failed to return. Halifax MZ831/*KW-Z* was one of sixteen aircraft despatched by No.425 (RCAF) Squadron, Tholthorpe. Its crew consisted of: Flying Officer Donald Smith (pilot); Flying Officer LS 'Jamie' Jamieson (navigator); Flying Officer Ervine Knorr (bomb-aimer); Flight Sergeant Wallace Clowes RAF (flight engineer); Sergeant Bob Ford (wireless operator); Sergeant Al Limacher (mid-upper gunner); and Sergeant Jim Gale (rear gunner). Most of the losses on the Bochum raid were attributable to nightfighters, but Halifax MZ831/*KW-Z* was caught by flak.

The crew of 'Smitty's Kite' had a largely uneventful trip to Bochum. However, they ran into trouble just as they were making their bombing run over the target, when an 88mm shell exploded close to the starboard inner engine. Peter Clowes, a distant relative of the flight engineer, has described what happened next:

Wallace Clowes' grave, Reichwald war cemetery, near Kleve.
(*Peter Clowes*)

'There was instant chaos among the crew on the flight deck when the shell hit them. Shrapnel ripped through the starboard side of the plane, shattering parts of the pilot's instrument panel and striking Flight Sergeant Clowes in his side. He slumped to the floor behind the pilot's seat. "Because he was standing beside me he prevented the shell splinters from hitting me," said Smith later. "Otherwise I doubt that I would have survived."

The exploding shell completely wrecked the starboard inner engine. Controls to much of the right-hand side of the aircraft were severed and

Sergeant Wallace Clowes. (Peter Clowes*)*

within seconds flames spread in a raging blur from one of the fuel tanks to the whole of the trailing edge of the wing. Automatic fire extinguishers failed to work. The navigator ripped a hand extinguisher off the side but that was of no use either. Smith tried turning off the master fuel cock and feathering the affected engine; again, the push-button switches failed to operate. By this time the starboard wing was an inferno of bright red and yellow flame.

Smith, aware that their full bomb load was still on board, flashed the emergency light signal and ordered everyone to grab their parachute packs and bale out. Jamieson yanked open the lower hatch and jumped, followed closely by Ford, the wireless operator. Knorr, who scrambled back from the nose, said afterwards: "We were in a serious irrecoverable situation. The last thing I remember is sitting on the edge of the hatch ready to leave. When I came to I was on my way down, my parachute opening at appoximately 5,000ft.

In the aircraft's tail the rear gunner, Flight Sergeant Gale, heard his captain's 'Bale out' order at the same time as he saw the starboard wing erupt into flame. He spun his turret around and dropped into the night sky. The shock of the exploding shell temporarily stunned Al Limacher... in the mid upper turret..., but he swiftly recovered as the flames licked towards him. He stepped down into the body of the plane and snapped on his parachute pack.

Smith, having seen three of his crew disappear through the floor hatch and assuming that the others would also be baling out, now attempted to fly the plane over the target. In some confused but dutiful way he was thinking that he could jettison the bombs then fly around into an area beyond Bochum that might be clear of flak before jumping himself. But the situation changed at lightning speed. The plane began to rock violently. Smith wrapped both arms around the control column and jammed his knees on the dash. But the control column hurled him back and forth helplessly and he was unable to prevent the plane going into a fatal spin. Then there was a mighty explosion and the young pilot felt his head smash into the instrument panel.

The blast ripped the Halifax apart in the area of the mid-upper turret. Twisted cables and other debris surrounded Limacher's feet and trapped him before he could jump clear. But, with great presence of mind, the gunner pulled his ripcord as he leaned out of the mid escape hatch. The 'chute opened, caught in the wind and snatched him clear of the corkscrewing plane.

The explosion that made Limacher's escape possible also probably saved his pilot's life. Luckily, Smith never fastened his seat harnes, except for take-off and landing. He was blown through the roof of the plane with his helmet, oxygen mask and earphones still attached. "I assume I hit something on the way out, otherwise I would have gone through the side and into the spinning propellors."

When Smith came to he was clear of the plane and falling swiftly. "I could not feel the usual heavy weight of a parachute and I thought at first that it was not attached to me. I was semi-conscious for a time but eventually realized that the 'chute was there. When

1944. No.425 (Alouette) Squadron Halifaxes at Tholthorpe. (via Peter Clowes)

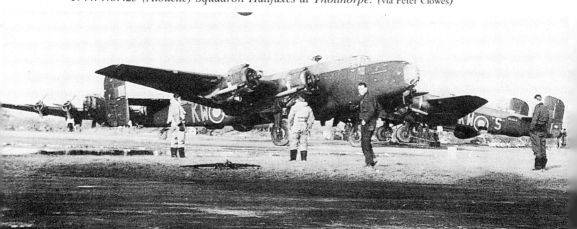

The survivors of the crash of No.425 Squadron Halifax MX831/KW-Z
(L-R): Sergeant Jim Gale (rear gunner); Sergeant Al Limacher (mid-upper gunner);
Flying Officer Ervine Knorr (bomb aimer); Flying Officer Jamie Jamieson (navigator);
Sergeant Bob Ford (wireless operator); Flying Officer Don Smith (pilot) (via Peter Clowes)

I tried to pull the ripcord, however, I found that my right arm was not functioning properly. It was rotating in a strange way and was, in fact, broken. I tried to pull the ripcord with my left hand but it was difficult because the upper portion of my flying gloves had blown over my thumb and fingers.

Smith had now plunged more than 12,000ft. After a further desperate struggle he finally managed to hook a finger into the ripcord ring and open his parachute. He was not far above the ground and the resulting heavy fall when he landed...broke one of his ribs'.

All of the Canadians landed safely and all were destined to spend the rest of the war as prisoners. The flight engineer was the only person not to survive the demise of MZ831.

'In the pandemonium on the flight deck no one had seen Flight Sergeant Wally Clowes since he slumped to the floor just behind the pilot's seat. They (later) rightly assumed that their English colleague and friend had been killed instantly and had been carried down in the crashing plane...'

The body of Wallace Clowes was recovered from the wreckage of his aircraft and was buried in the war cemetery at Kleve, forty-five miles north-west of Bochum and close by the Dutch-German border.

'Four German gardeners — all war veterans — keep the adjacent lawns and flower beds as neat and tidy as a palace garden. There are some 3,000 other graves in that section of the cemetery. All are of Allied airmen who died, like Wallace Clowes, over the Ruhr fifty years ago'.

RCAF Middleton-St-George 31 May, 1945. Air Chief Marshal Sir AT 'Bomber' Harris, Chief of Bomber Command, addresses RCAF crews and ground staff prior to their departure for Canada. Following the speech, the first fifteen Canadian-built Lancaster bombers of No.428 Ghost Squadron left for home.

'Exactly at 10.15 the planes of "Ghost Squadron" were ready to take off. The crews had been previously addressed by Air Chief Marshal Sir Arthur Harris, C-in-C Bomber Command and Air Marshal GO Johnson, OC of the RCAF Overseas.

Straight away they dashed for the planes and at a given signal, the engines were "revved" up and Wing Commander Gall of Lachute, Quebec, who has sixty-five operational trips to his credit led the parade of the bombers.

His plane rose beautifully into the air and at one minute intervals the fourteen other bombers followed. After circling round the 'drome and in some cases dropping coloured flares, they started their homeward flight.

As each bomber swept along the runway, hundreds of WAAFS and members of the ground staff wished all the crews "Good Luck". They cheered and waved their caps and the RAF band played topical music, which included *The Maple Leaf, O Canada, Auld Lang Syne.*

They were the first flight, and from today onwards fifteen planes a day will be leaving until all aircrews have gone. Ground crews will be following by sea.'

(*Middlesbrough* Evening Gazette *31 May, 1945*)

Middleton-St-George, 15 May, 1945. Lancaster bombers of No.428 (Ghost) Squadron, RCAF prepare to leave for home. In this picture NA-F leads NA-G. If Bill McMullen had not crashed in NA-E at Darlington on 13 January, 1945, he might well have been leading this particular line-up. (via AJR 'Robbie' Robson)

Postscript

DORMANSTOWN (CLEVELAND) LANCASTER

17 December, 1942

RAF operations for the night of 17/18 December, 1942, included the despatching of fifty aircraft to lay mines along a broad front stretching from Denmark to southern Biscay.

No.101 (Lancaster) Squadron, Holme-on-Spalding Moor, was detailed to provide six aircraft, one of which was Lancaster Mk B1 (W4319) coded *SR-N*. Its composite crew consisted of Sergeant Alec Fussell RAF (pilot); Sergeant Jack Worsnop RAF (flight engineer); Sergeant Sidney McClean RNZAF (bomb aimer); Sergeant Monte McIntyre RNZAF (wireless operator); Sergeant James O'Malley RNZAF (air gunner); Sergeant Gregory Georges RCAF (air gunner); and Sergeant George Warren RAF (air gunner).

They were young. With the exceptions of McIntyre and McClean — both 'old men' at the age of twenty-nine years — they were hardly out of school. Fussell, the captain of the aircraft, was twenty years old — just one year older than Warren; O'Malley, Georges and Worsnop were twenty-one, twenty-two and twenty-three years of age respectively.

Weather conditions over the North Sea were not good and because of 10/10ths cloud (which persisted down to sea level in some areas), a number of crews aborted their task. Fussell, however, persisted and subsequently laid his six mines off Heligoland before setting course for home.

While the RAF bombers were sowing their mines, the *Luftwaffe's Kampfgeschwader 2* was launching an attack against York which was to cost them two Dornier 217 bombers. One crashed on Wheeldale Moor, above Goathland in bad weather after, so it is believed, having been struck by anti-aircraft fire as it crossed in near Whitby; the other was the victim of low-flying and poor weather conditions and struck a hill at Crow Nest, near the Bilsdale village of Hawnby.

Whether by accident or design, enemy aircraft were also operating over the coastal strip further north that night. The Redcar 'Alert' sounded at 21.52hrs, some sixteen minutes before incendiary bombs fell near the *Starfish* decoy site south of Sandy Lane, New Marske — and some eighteen minutes before Fussell made his landfall close by the Warrenby Ironworks, just south of the river Tees. The Lancaster was off track and fifty miles north of where it should have been. In addition, Its IFF[1] was

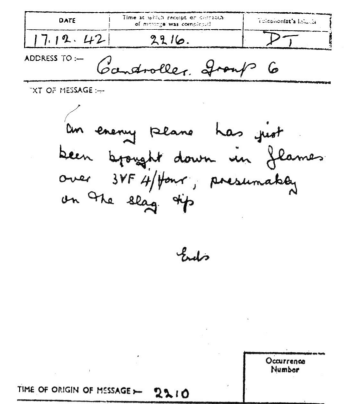

DATE	Time at which receipt or despatch of message was completed	Telephonist's Initials
17.12.42	2216.	DT

ADDRESS TO :— *Controller. Group 6*

TEXT OF MESSAGE :—

An enemy plane has just been brought down in flames over 3VF 4/Hour, presumably on the slag tip

Ends

Occurrence Number

TIME OF ORIGIN OF MESSAGE :— **2210**

ADDRESS FROM :— *Redcar*

The message that recorded the demise of Lancaster SR-N at Dormanstown on the night of 17 December, 1942.

not working. Thus, when the returning bomber was picked up by British radar, it was assumed to be hostile.

It was flying at some 250ft as it banked over Warrenby Ironworks and when a searchlight picked it out, the crew of the Bofors gun sited on a 70ft tower in the centre of the plant could hardly miss. The unmistakable sound of the Bofors — a heavy rat-tat-tat, like an outsized machine-gun — sent a continuous stream of 40mm two-pounder explosive shells into the air. Three of them struck the Lancaster and, in the words of an eye-witness, '...blew it out of the sky...' The bomber crashed close to what is now Steel House, Dormanstown: there were no survivors.

With the exceptions of Alec Fussell and Jack Worsnop, whose burial place is unknown, the crew was buried in Acklam Road cemetery, Thornaby, where they still lie.

They have no public memorial other than their gravestone.

---

[1] All British aircraft were equipped with an IFF (Identification — Friend or Foe) transmitting device which was operated when within British radar range. When activated, it gave a distinctive periodic elongation to the blip produced on a radar screen by an approaching aircraft and thus enabled defenders to distinguish friendly aircraft from hostile.

BIBLIOGRAPHY

Adams, W/O CW DFM: *578 Squadron Operations, 1944-45* Privately published 1994

Anon: *A History of 426 (Thunderbird) Squadron, RCAF* (an undated monograph obtained via Bill Michenor, UK Rep. 426 (Thunderbird) Squadron Association)

Anon: *The Royal Canadian Air Force at Linton-on-Ouse, 1942-1945* (undated monograph pub by RAF Linton-on-Ouse)

Anon: *434 Squadron History* Hangar Bookshelf, Canada, 1984

Anon: *The RCAF Overseas: the first four years* Oxford University Press, Toronto 1944

Ball, Harry: *Two Brothers at War* Janus 1992

Bomber Command Association *Newsletter* No.21 October 1992; No.22 February 1993

C.A.H.S Journal the Canadian Aviation Historical Society June 1984

Cassels, Ron: *Ghost Squadron* Ardenlea Pub. Canada 1991

Cawdron, Hugh: *Based at Burn* Privately Pub. 1995

Charlwood, Don: *No Moon Tonight* Goodall Pubs. edition 1987

Chorley, WR: *In Brave Company* (No.158 Squadron Operations) Privately published 1990 ed

Dunmore, S/Carter,W: *Reap the Whirlwind* (the untold story of No.6 Group, Canada's bomber force of World War II) McClelland & Stewart, Canada 1991

Elmer, V: *The Moose Squadron* unpub MSS Canada 1987 (via Sheila Barnett)

Emmett, Norman *One Foot on the Ground* Lugus Pubs. Canada 1992

Ford, K: *Snaith Days* (life with No.51 Squadron, 1942-45) No.51 Squadron Association 1993

Halpenny, Bruce Barrymore: *Action Stations; 4* (military airfields of Yorkshire) Patrick Stephens 1982

Halpenny, Bruce Barrymore: *To Shatter the Sky:* (bomber airfield at war) Patrick Stephens 1984

Hastings, Max: *Bomber Command* Book Club Associates 1980

Jefford, C.G. MBE W/Cdr: *RAF Squadrons* (a comprehensive record of the movement and equipment of all RAF squadrons and their antecedents since 1912) Airlife 1988

Jones, Geoffrey: *Raider: the Halifax and its Flyers* Kimber 1978

Lunn, B/Arbon, L: *Aircraft Down III* (RAF Riccall and No.1658 HCU) Hardwick Pubs, Pontefract 1989

Middlebrook, Martin/Everitt, Chris: *The Bomber Command War Diaries* Penguin ed. 1990

Middlebrook, Martin: *The Berlin Raids* Viking 1988

Middlesbrough Evening Gazette, 31 May 1945

Parry, Simon W: *Intruders over Britain* (the Luftwaffe night fighter offensive, 1940-45). Air Research Pubs. 1987

Pocklington Post Publishing: *G-George* Supplement (Colin Stokoe/James Houston) March 1993

Rames, Georges; 'All in a night's work' in *Air Clues Magazine* December 1984

Sawyer, Tom Group Captain DFC: *Only Owls and Bloody Fools Fly at Night* Goodall Pubs ed. 1985

Selby Times 12 May, 1944; 19 May, 1944.

Smith, AC; *Halifax Crew* (the story of a wartime bomber crew) 2nd ed. Yorkshire Air Museum 1987

No.10 Squadron Association *Newsletter* Autumn 1985 and Winter 1992

Thurston, R: 'Baling out over Berlin' in *Intercom* (Aircrew Association) Autumn 1988

Todd, AAB: *Pilgrimages of Grace*; a history of Croft aerodrome, Alan Todd Associates 1993

Public Record Office:
No.10 Squadron: AIR 27/143
No.51 Squadron: AIR 24/269
No.76 Squadron: AIR 27/651
No.77 Squadron: AIR 14/3410; AIR 27/656
No.78 Squadron: AIR 27/660; AIR 14/2673
No.102 (Ceylon) Squadron: AIR 27/809
No.158 Squadron: AIR 27/1048; AIR 27/1049
No.419 (Moose) Squadron: AIR 27/1823; AIR 28 (M-S-G);
No.428 (Ghost) Squadron: AIR 27/1850
No.429 (Bison) Squadron: AIR 28/61; AIR 27/1853
No.466 Squadron RAAF: 27/1926